City of London
TIMELINE

City of London
TIMELINE

SARA PINK

The
History
Press

First published 2016

The History Press
The Mill, Brimscombe Port
Stroud, Gloucestershire, GL5 2QG
www.thehistorypress.co.uk

British Library Cataloguing in Publication Data.
A catalogue record for this book is available from the British Library.

ISBN 978 0 7509 6843 0

Design by Chris West
Printed in Turkey by Imak

About the Author

Sara Pink is the Head of Guildhall and City Business Libraries at the City of London Corporation. She has a degree in History and is studying for a Masters in the History of the Book at the University of London. She lives in Buckinghamshire with her husband David and their four cats, and has a passion for travel, horses and all things London.

Acknowledgements

The support of the City of London Corporation in the work involved in producing this book is gratefully acknowledged.

All the staff who contributed ideas to this book were involved in the selection of material and their efforts are much appreciated. The photography for this book was undertaken by the Image & Media staff at London Metropolitan Archives.

List of Contributors

Nick Bodger
Andrew Brown
Tim Chapman
Jeff Cook
Valerie Hart
Sheldon Hind
Stuart Millar
Leanne O'Boyle
Peter Ross
Laurence Ward

Image Credits

Front cover: Olympics © Clive Totman
Front cover: Gherkin © Jamie Smith
122: Hadrian, Wikimedia Commons, FollowingHadrian
290: Wikimedia Commons, Numismatica Ars Classica NAC AG
851: Model of the Gokstad ship, Wikimedia Commons, Softeis
962: Flaming Torch © Andrew Dunn, 5 November 2005
1814: Thames Frost Fair, Wikimedia Commons, Thomas Wyke
1888: Jack the Ripper Victim © *The Illustrated Police News*
1986: Lloyds Building, Wikimedia Commons, User:Colin
2002: Golden Jubilee © Jamie Smith
2004: The Gherkin © Jamie Smith
2007: City of London Information Centre © Jamie Smith
2011: Protestors occupy St Paul's © Jamie Smith
2012: Olympic and Paralympic Games © Clive Totman

ROMAN LONDON

The road to Dubris

The Romans' legendary road-building skills are employed from an early date, and roads soon connect Londinium to Lindum (Lincoln), Eboracum (York) and Dubris (Dover). Today we know these roads as Bishopsgate (the road to Lincoln and York) and Watling Street (the road to Dover).

41-43

50-70

We shall call it Londinium

Almost 100 years after their first invasion in 55 BC the Romans return, and a settlement, Londinium, is established on the site of modern-day London. Within twenty years Londinium prospers sufficiently to be described by Tacitus in his Annals as 'a busy centre, chiefly through its crowd of merchants and stores'.

Amphitheatre of life and death

A wooden amphitheatre is built in the area now covered by Guildhall Yard. The walls are rebuilt in stone in 120 and the arena is used for military drills, religious ceremonies, animal fights, the execution of criminals and gladiatorial combat.

60/61

80

75

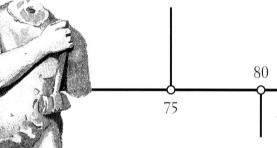

Boudicca burns London

Boudicca, Queen of the Iceni, attacks the Romans because of the mistreatment of her family and people. Together with the Trinovantes tribe she destroys Camulodunum (Colchester), and then proceeds to lay waste to London and its bridge. She is eventually defeated in battle by the Romans and commits suicide.

Governor of Britain's headquarters

The headquarters of the Procurator of the province of Britannia are built between 80 and 100 where Cannon Street Station now stands. It is believed that London Stone may simply have been a post at the gates of this palace, a marker for distances from London.

Fort built in Cripplegate

The City Wall, built at the end of the second century, incorporates within its circuit the already existing fort in the north-west corner of the City at Cripplegate.

122

c. 100

Emperor Hadrian visits Londinium

This follows a period of major rebellion in the province of Britannia from 119 to 121.

Londinium destroyed by fire

Over 100 acres, a fifth of
the City, is destroyed by
flames from a probably
accidental fire. Many see this
as an opportunity to rebuild
anew and extend the City.

c. 190-225

125

The Great Wall

Late in the 2nd century the Romans begin
building a wall around the perimeter of
the City. The wall is nearly 3 miles long,
20ft high and 8ft thick. It originally has
five gates: Ludgate, Newgate, Cripplegate,
Bishopsgate and Aldgate. The gate at
Aldersgate is added in *c.* 350 and another
at Moorgate during the medieval period.

Aldersgate

Bridges

London began with a bridge, although nobody knows exactly when. Certainly a good place to cross the River Thames was the first reason for our city's existence back in the 1st century AD. And that first bridge, London Bridge, rebuilt numerous times over the centuries in wood, stone and most recently concrete, inspiration for Norse poetry and nursery rhymes, has been at the centre of London's life since its inception.

The medieval bridge, with its nineteen brick arches, covered in houses with a roadway squeezed in the middle, was a marvel of Gothic architecture, but was prone to fall to bits from the power of the tidal Thames, and so required constant upkeep, paid for from countless legacies, wills and donations of land to 'God and the Bridge'. These were sufficiently numerous that funds from the Bridge House Trust paid for the construction of William Pitt Bridge, which you've never heard of because it's always been known as Blackfriars Bridge, and the same body is responsible for maintenance of Southwark Bridge, the Millennium Bridge, and the most well-known of all, Tower Bridge.

If you want to see how London Bridge used to look, you'll have to seek out the church of St Magnus the Martyr at its north end, where they have a scale model of the medieval bridge. Or you'll have to go to Arizona, where its 19th-century replacement ended up.

Although London Bridge was the capital's only bridge for over 1,700 years and bears the famous name, it isn't the bridge people think of when they imagine London. That honour goes to Tower Bridge, a relative minnow at only 120 years old, a unique combination of engineering nous and Victorian civic pride.

Tower Bridge was the 19th-century answer to a problem – how to build a bridge that people can cross over and ships can pass through all at the same time? And the solution, arrived at after competitions and committee meetings and years of indecision, was a medieval one. A drawbridge. Admittedly under the stone skin was pure Victorian muscle, steam-powered bascules and steel suspension cables, but it looked medieval all the same, both in deference to the nearby Tower of London, and because neo-Gothic was the fashion at the time.

The bridge opened in 1894, and although the end of London's riverside trade in the late 20th century rendered this double role a little redundant, Tower Bridge has refound its purpose as a popular tourist attraction with terrific views upriver, downriver, and most recently straight down to the river, with the installation of glass-panelled floors in the walkways.

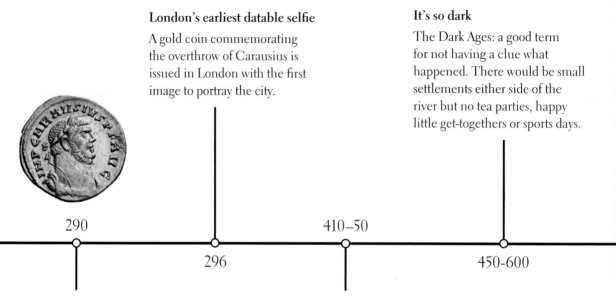

London's earliest datable selfie

A gold coin commemorating the overthrow of Carausius is issued in London with the first image to portray the city.

It's so dark

The Dark Ages: a good term for not having a clue what happened. There would be small settlements either side of the river but no tea parties, happy little get-togethers or sports days.

290

296

410–50

450-600

London minted

Carausius, pretender to the Imperial Roman throne, emphasises his independence by setting up the first mint. Gold, silver and copper coins washed with silver are issued.

Romans abandon

In the face of threats to Rome itself, and despite a plea for protection from his subjects in Britain, the Emperor Honorius decides not to send any troops to defend the province. Londinium is abandoned, possibly from a lack of sufficient manpower to garrison the walls, and by the mid-5th century the Roman settlement falls silent.

SAXON
LONDON

St Paul's Cathedral

The first of five cathedrals to be built on this site is
founded in the reign of Ethelbert, King of Kent,
the first Christian king in England. Mellitus,
a monk who accompanies St Augustine
to Britain, orders the building of a
cathedral dedicated to St Paul.

604

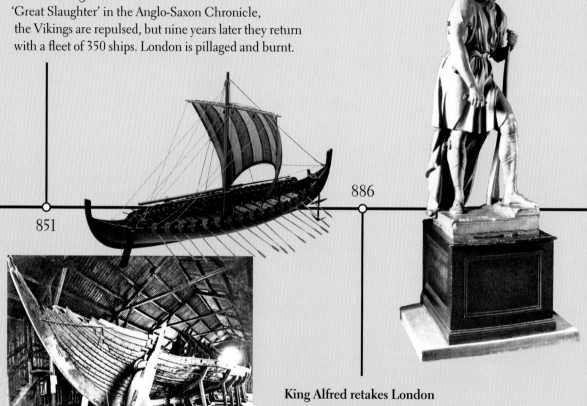

The Vikings are coming!

In 842 Vikings attack London. Recorded as a
'Great Slaughter' in the Anglo-Saxon Chronicle,
the Vikings are repulsed, but nine years later they return
with a fleet of 350 ships. London is pillaged and burnt.

851

886

King Alfred retakes London

Alfred the Great captures London from the
Danes, reoccupying the old walled City that
has been largely deserted since the Romans left.

City Sayings

There are lots of fascinating sayings in common usage that have their origins in the ancient City of London. There is often quite a bit of disagreement about where these sayings come from.

Sent to Coventry – meaning to be ostracised, this comes from people literally being sent to Coventry. If a trader or livery company misbehaved in the City of London, their permission to operate in the City was revoked, meaning they had to go to the nearest town with a market – Coventry – to earn their living.

Sixes and sevens – meaning to be in some sort of disorder, and – legend has it – stemming from the arrangement of the Great Twelve livery companies whose order of precedence was a matter of honour. The companies of the Merchant Taylors and the Skinners couldn't agree on their places in the order, so it was resolved to swap each year: one would be six and the other seven, and vice versa the next year.

Floats – meaning a display vehicle in a parade or pageant. This term comes from the Lord Mayor's Show: the procession originally took place on the River Thames, and so the decorated barges that took part were named 'floats'. The name stuck when the Show moved to dry land.

Baker's dozen – bakers traditionally sold items in batches of 13 for the price of 12; this is because the sale of baked goods was heavily regulated by the Worshipful Company of Bakers. Punishments for under-selling were severe, so bakers included an extra loaf to be on the safe side.

Dick Whittington's cat – popularised in the pantomime story of the four-time Mayor of London, Dick's cat wasn't actually a cat. It was a barge – a very important thing for a merchant to have – which was nicknamed a 'cat' in medieval times. We have no knowledge of whether or not Dick Whittington owned a feline.

Hear a pin drop – meaning a very quiet situation. This comes from the tea auctions in the east of the City, which used to be done 'by candle'. A pin was stuck into a lighted candle an inch from the top, and the last bid to be heard before the pin fell out was the winner. If no one bid, you could hear a pin drop.

On the wagon – meaning someone who abstains from alcohol. Its gruesome origins allegedly lie in the practise of giving condemned men a drink at the local pub before they were taken by wagon from Newgate Prison to Tyburn to be hanged. If someone offered the prisoner a second drink, the escort would decline – the man was going on the wagon.

First mention of London Bridge

According to the Anglo-Saxon Chronicle, a widow charged with witchcraft is punished by being drowned in the Thames at London Bridge. This is the first mention of a bridge since Roman times.

962

975

St Paul's burns

The Vikings light a fire which destroys St Paul's Cathedral as a plague fever sweeps the city.

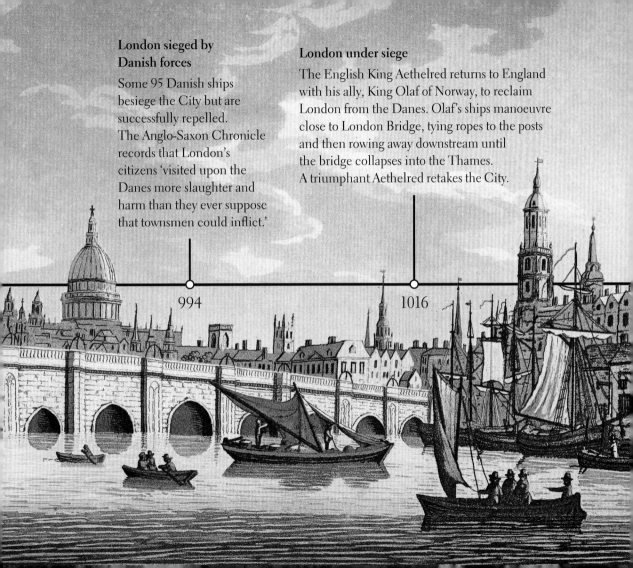

London sieged by Danish forces

Some 95 Danish ships besiege the City but are successfully repelled. The Anglo-Saxon Chronicle records that London's citizens 'visited upon the Danes more slaughter and harm than they ever suppose that townsmen could inflict.'

994

London under siege

The English King Aethelred returns to England with his ally, King Olaf of Norway, to reclaim London from the Danes. Olaf's ships manoeuvre close to London Bridge, tying ropes to the posts and then rowing away downstream until the bridge collapses into the Thames. A triumphant Aethelred retakes the City.

1016

NORMAN & MEDIEVAL LONDON

1067

Conqueror's charter

Following his victory at Hastings in 1066, William the Conqueror is crowned King in Westminster Abbey. In a charter written in Anglo-Saxon he grants the City of London the right to the freedoms and independence that the citizens of London had enjoyed under Edward the Confessor. Preserved at Guildhall, this unique document is still the basis of many City privileges.

Gundulf's White Tower

Gundulf, Bishop of Rochester, supervises the building of the White Tower in Caen stone. At the time it is the largest non-religious building in the country. Taking more than twenty years to complete, it is 90ft high with walls up to 15ft thick. It is to serve as a palace, a treasury and a stronghold guarding the river entrance into the City. It also contains the oldest toilet in London.

1078

Thomas Becket

Chancellor and later Archbishop of Canterbury, Becket's quarrels with Henry II over the respective powers of Church and State lead to his murder in Canterbury Cathedral in 1170. Canonised in 1173, his shrine becomes a place of pilgrimage from all over Europe.

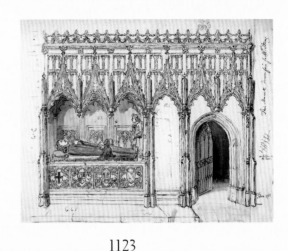

1091

c. 1118

1123

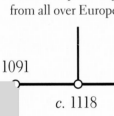

The windy city

Britain's earliest recorded tornado strikes on 17 October 1091, killing two people in London. London Bridge is destroyed, together with many of London's churches and over 600 houses.

St Bart's

St Bartholomew's, the oldest hospital in London, is founded by Rahere, a clergyman, courtier, minstrel and jester. On a pilgrimage to Rome, he falls ill with malaria and has a vision of St Bartholomew, telling him to found a hospital. On his return to England he builds a church, St Bartholomew's, which also has a separate wing dedicated to the care of the sick.

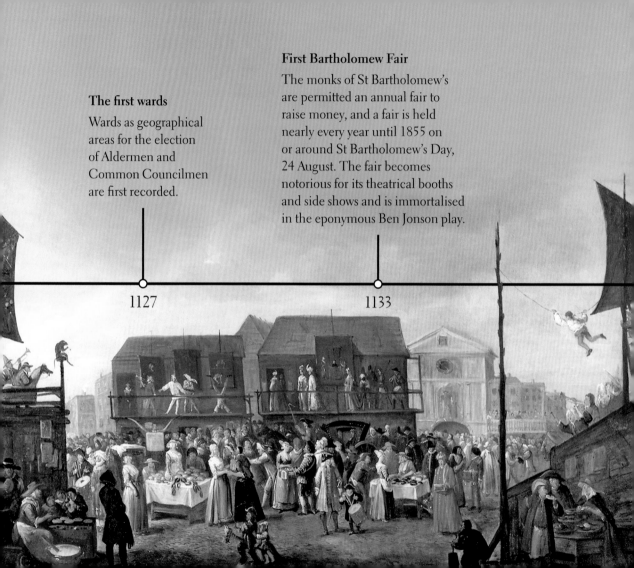

The first wards

Wards as geographical areas for the election of Aldermen and Common Councilmen are first recorded.

First Bartholomew Fair

The monks of St Bartholomew's are permitted an annual fair to raise money, and a fair is held nearly every year until 1855 on or around St Bartholomew's Day, 24 August. The fair becomes notorious for its theatrical booths and side shows and is immortalised in the eponymous Ben Jonson play.

1127

1133

Geoffrey of Monmouth writes dubious history

Much of the source material for legends relating to the foundation of London comes from Geoffrey's *History of the Kings of Britain*, including the notion that London was founded by refugees from Troy and the country was populated by a race of giants, including the famous Gogmagog.

Medieval Hasselhoff

William Fitzstephen writes a detailed, although subjective, description of London in the preface to his biography of Thomas Becket. In his opinion, 'The only problems that plague London are the idiots who drink to excess and the frequency of fires.' His text is the first in England to mention football and references Knightrider Street, which legend has it takes its name from the knights who would process from the Tower of London to the jousts. Today, Knightrider Street is popular with fans of David Hasselhoff.

1155

1136

1174

The first craft guild

The Weavers' Company becomes the first of the chartered craft guilds in the City.

McLEAN'S MONTHLY SHEET OF CARICATURES Nº 25.

GRAND COMBAT BETWEEN THE CITY CHAMPIONS GOG AND MAGOG.

London Bridge is falling down

Work starts on a stone crossing of the Thames, replacing the existing wooden bridge. Spanning 900ft of tidal water, it takes 33 years to complete but lasts into the 19th century.

The Da Vinci Code

The medieval circular Temple Church is built by the Knights Templar to a design based on the Church of the Holy Sepulchre in Jerusalem. The church still houses the graves of a number of Knights Templar, and is featured in the book (and later film) *The Da Vinci Code*.

1176

1185

The unofficial Mayor

The City of London is officially granted the right to have its own Mayor by King John in 1215, but the post actually predates this. Henry Fitz-Ailwin, the first Mayor (today known as the Lord Mayor) is believed to have held the position from 1189–1212, initially under John's predecessor, Richard the Lionheart.

City friaries

During the 13th century a new monastic order – friars – establish houses in the City: the Franciscans (Grey Friars) near Newgate; the Dominicans (Black Friars) first in Holborn but later in the area south of St Paul's, and the Carmelites (White Friars) south of Fleet Street. Also in the City are the Austin Friars (Augustinians), Crossed (Crutched) Friars, and the Order of St Clare (Minoresses).

1189

1200

1212

Another disastrous fire

A fire breaks out in Southwark and spreads to London Bridge, leading to the death of around 3,000 people and the loss of the chapel and many houses on the bridge. A law is subsequently passed decreeing that all new buildings be built with stone walls and tiled roofs, although many older timber buildings still remain.

Gog and Magog

Chief among the visitor attractions at Guildhall are the two wooden figures standing sentinel by the gallery at the west end of the Great Hall; 9ft 3in in height, and carved from limewood by David Evans, these are Gog and Magog, the Guildhall Giants. Both wear Roman armour and laurel crowns, but Gog carries a staff from which hangs a chain and spiked ball, and has a sword and quiver of arrows, while Magog holds a halberd and a shield with a phoenix relief. This latest incarnation of the giants was unveiled on 8 June 1953, the gift of Alderman Sir George Wilkinson, but such figures have a long history, stretching back through medieval pageants to the legendary race of giants once thought to have inhabited Britain.

Although giants had taken part in City pageants since the 15th century, they were anonymous figures, probably constructed only as occasion demanded, so never accrued an individual identity. However, in 1554 and 1558, the giants taking part in London festivities were named as Corineus the Briton and Gogmagog the Albion. Somewhere in the evolution from pageant figures to more permanent guardians of the City, the name Corineus was forgotten, and his companion's name was divided between the two giants.

It is not known when these figures first took up residence in Guildhall, but most sources suggest that the giants were destroyed during the Great Fire of 1666. By 1672 replacement figures, 15ft high and probably made of wicker and plasterboard, were being set up in Guildhall. Time and the depredations of rats and mice led to their replacement in 1708. Carved by Richard Saunders of King Street, Cheapside at a cost of £70, the new Gog and Magog were made of firwood and were 14ft 6in in height. Originally erected on the north side of Guildhall flanking the entrance to the Council Chamber, they were removed to their present position in 1815. These figures were destroyed by enemy action on 29 December 1940.

Saunders' wooden giants would have been too heavy to take part in the Lord Mayor's Show, but in 1827 two wickerwork figures 14ft high, depicting Gog and Magog, walked in the Mayor's procession. In 2006 the two giants, recreated in willow by members of the Basketmakers' Company, once more graced the Lord Mayor's Show.

Mayoral charter

To secure its support, King John grants the City the right to elect its own Mayor, thereby confirming one of the first elected offices in the modern world. To temper this power base, the Charter also stipulates that the new Mayor must swear an oath of allegiance to the Sovereign and be 'shown' to the people, a tradition that continues to this day as the Lord Mayor's Show.

1215

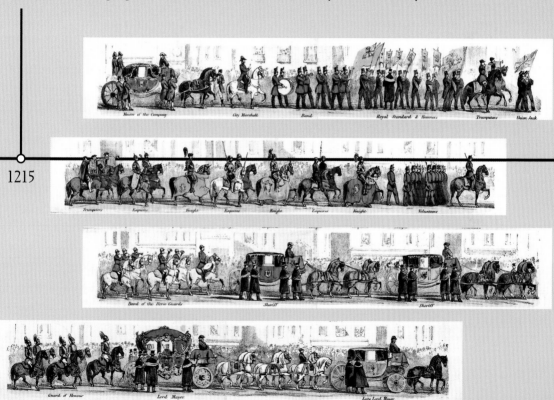

The right to a fair trial

A posse of barons air their grievances with King John at Temple. The King commits to an agreement, which becomes the precious document Magna Carta. The City's Magna Carta links don't end there: the City is explicitly mentioned in Magna Carta, and is now custodian of the finest remaining 13th-century charter.

1215

The City and Magna Carta

Magna Carta remains one of the most important documents in democratic history. A milestone in the development of the rule of law, it curtailed royal power and established rules and rights that increased the liberty of free men.

The City of London played an active role in the events that led to its creation and the Mayor (later known as the Lord Mayor) was appointed, along with the barons, to see that its provisions were carried out.

The story begins with 'Bad King John' who, on losing lands in France that were under his rule, waged expensive wars to win them back (which he failed to do). To pay for the wars he increased taxes – a move that unsettled some of England's most powerful barons and threatened a full-scale civil war. In early 1215, the barons confronted John at Temple and negotiations began which led to the sealing of Magna Carta on 15 June 1215.

Shortly before, John tried to get the City on side by issuing the Mayoral Charter, which allowed it the right to elect its own mayor (though it had already been doing so for at least twenty-five years). The attempt failed, and the City sided with the barons – a move resulting in London being the only place to be specifically named in Magna Carta in a clause stating that 'the City of London shall have all its ancient liberties by land as well as by water'.

In the 13th century, new Kings reissued Magna Carta during political negotiations, and copies were sent out to regional sheriffs across the country. The City of London still holds a 13th-century edition – considered one of the finest in existence. It is periodically on public display at the City's Heritage Gallery in Guildhall Art Gallery.

Prince Louis of France

Prince Louis, heir to the French throne, invades southern England and is proclaimed King of England in St Paul's Cathedral. However, on the death of King John later this year, most of Louis's supporters desert him in favour of John's 9-year-old son, Henry III.

'Quit Rent Services': a very curious tradition

Blacksmith Walter le Burn opens his forge near the Strand in 1235; the annual rent is to be 6 horseshoes and 61 nails. Later, the City of London Corporation acquire this land, and the City Solicitor still pays the appropriate rent to the Queen's Remembrancer in an annual ceremony. Every year, the 'rent' is given back to the Corporation so that it can be used in the following year's ceremony. The same horseshoes and nails have been exchanging hands for over 600 years.

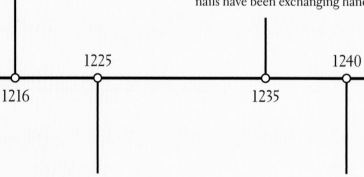

1216

1225

1235

1240

Greyfriars monastery

Franciscan friars establish a monastic house in the heart of the City's butchery district (in a street until recently called Stinking Lane) to minister directly to the spiritual needs of the people of London.

St Paul's spire

The new wooden spire that tops St Paul's is probably high enough at 489ft to qualify as the tallest manmade structure in the world at this time.

First record of Paul's Cross

The preaching cross in the churchyard of St Paul's Cathedral is the site of mass public meetings, royal proclamations, heretic burnings and regular sermons.

1245

1241

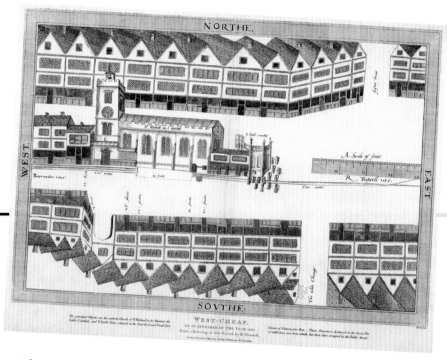

Great conduit built in Cheapside

To bring fresh water to the heavily populated City, springs are purchased in Paddington in 1237, pipes laid, and a cistern constructed in Cheapside that supplies this area with fresh water for over 400 years. The location is lost after the Great Fire, found by accident in both 1899 and 1994, and is finally commemorated with a plaque on the pavement in 2014.

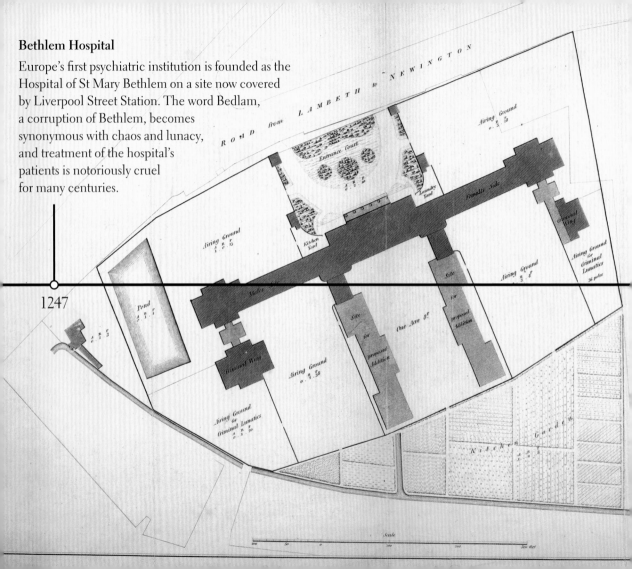

Bethlem Hospital

Europe's first psychiatric institution is founded as the Hospital of St Mary Bethlem on a site now covered by Liverpool Street Station. The word Bedlam, a corruption of Bethlem, becomes synonymous with chaos and lunacy, and treatment of the hospital's patients is notoriously cruel for many centuries.

1247

Earliest painted view of London

In Mathew Paris' itinerary for a pilgrimage (essentially a travel guide from London to Jerusalem) appears a view of London. St Paul's Cathedral, the Tower of London, the City wall and its gates, London Bridge and St Mary le Bow Church are depicted.

City is punished

Having chosen the losing side in the war between Henry III and Simon de Montfort, the City is fined £13,000 and suffers the temporary loss of its liberties.

1252

1255

1265

An elephant in the Tower

The first elephant ever seen in England arrives as a gift from Louis IX of France to King Henry III. The elephant joins other exotic animals, like a polar bear and leopards, in the menagerie at the Tower of London.

Animals in the City

When King Henry III was given three leopards by his new brother-in-law, Frederick, the Holy Roman Emperor, he ordered – in desperation – that they be sent to the Tower of London. John Stow records the arrival of the three leopards in his *Annals of London* available at Guildhall Library.

Soon after the arrival of the leopards in 1235 they were joined by a Norwegian polar bear in 1252. The Sheriffs of the City of London were told to provide money towards the bear's food and keep, but after a year or so of the expense the people of London were instructed to invest in a muzzle, chain and rope so that the bear could be kept on the bank of the Thames and could fish for his own food. The bear was encouraged to learn to fish for salmon just downstream of London Bridge.

In 1255 an elephant walked the long Canterbury–London road towards the capital and entered the City by boat up the Thames. It was a gift from the French King Louis IX which was a trophy from crusades against Palestine.

Over the next 600 years, the Tower of London played host to thousands more exotic creatures all brought from overseas by returning explorers or VIP guests.

William Blake came to look at the 'tygers' and John Wesley played his flute to the lions in an attempt to establish whether they had souls.

In 1436 there was an epidemic at the Tower Menagerie which carried off most of the animals.

The conduits run with wine

The day after Edward I is crowned, 'the Conduit in Chepe ran all the day with red and white wine to drink, for all such who wished.'

1272

1274

1275

Destruction of the Great Synagogue

There has been a Jewish community in London since William the Conqueror's time, living under royal protection but increasingly oppressed, taxed and attacked. The Great Synagogue is closed in 1272, and in 1290 the Jews are expelled. There is no official Jewish presence in England for 360 years.

Custom House built

The Custom House belonging to the Crown is first recorded in this year, situated on Lower Thames Street at the Old Wool Quay. England's most valuable commodity is its wool.

Steelyard

The powerful Baltic trading empire, the Hanseatic League, establish The Steelyard, a complex of buildings named after a steel-weighing beam in the courtyard, first recorded in 1157. The German merchants lose much power before the reign of Elizabeth I, but remain until 1863 when the site is demolished to build Cannon Street Station.

1281

Wallace's gruesome end

Scottish patriot William Wallace is sentenced to death for treason. His grisly end involves being dragged naked behind a horse from the Tower of London to Smithfield, then being hanged, emasculated, disembowelled (with his bowels then burnt in front of him), beheaded and then quartered. His head, dipped in tar, is placed on a pike atop London Bridge. A plaque on the wall of St Bartholomew's Hospital commemorates his death.

1282/83

1305

Well, a prison!

Henry Wallis, Mayor of London, orders the digging of a well in Cornhill and the building of a prison, which comes to be known as the Tun, next to it. The well, which still exists, is re-dug and a pump erected in 1799 by the neighbouring fire insurance companies. It's still there.

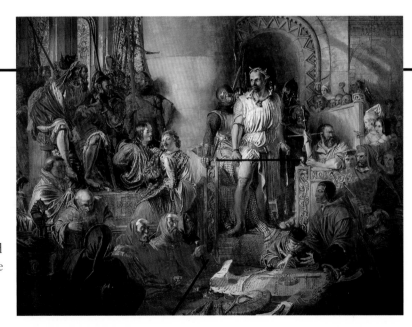

Black Death

The Black Death or plague arrives
in London in September 1348
and reaches its virulent zenith in
1349, wiping out whole families
and devastating friaries and
hospitals. The City churchyards
fill to overflowing and new burial
grounds have to be created beyond
the City walls. It is said there are
insufficient living to carry the dead.

1363

1348

Five kings

In the year that the Worshipful
Company of Vintners
(wine merchants) receives its
charter, the vintner and former
Lord Mayor Henry Picard
hosts five monarchs at a great
banquet: the King of England,
his prisoner the King of France,
and the Kings of Scotland,
Denmark and Cyprus.

Richard (Dick) Whittington, c. 1350–1423

A figure of popular legend and pantomime, the real Whittington was a major figure in the development of medieval London's government, its buildings and its society. Whittington was born in Gloucestershire around 1350, the son of a wealthy landowner. He became a London mercer, entering the lucrative trade in high-class materials including cloth of gold. He rapidly became a leading member of the trade and the Mercers' Guild, supplying luxury fabrics to the royal court. Diversifying into banking, he was so wealthy that he was eventually loaning money to Richard II, Henry IV and Henry V.

In 1384 Whittington became a Councilman. By 1393 he was an Alderman and that same year was appointed Sheriff by the incumbent Mayor William Standone. When Mayor Adam Bamme died in office in 1397, Whittington was imposed on the City as Lord Mayor by the King. However, Whittington quickly negotiated a deal with the King to buy back the City's liberties with the then enormous sum of £10,000; in thanks the City confirmed his appointment as Mayor by electing him to the post again in October of the same year. He was to be elected on two further occasions in 1406 and 1419 and became a Member of Parliament in 1416. But it is probably through the benefactions during his life and the bequests he left when he died a childless widower in 1423 that he is best remembered. Through the bequests and charitable works we can trace the founding of hospitals and almshouses, public lavatories, the rebuilding of Guildhall and of his parish church St Michael Paternoster Royal, Newgate Prison and the first incarnation of Guildhall Library. Unlike any other Londoner of his age, his fame has passed into popular culture and he is remembered today, even if only in pantomime, as Dick Whittington, thrice Mayor of London.

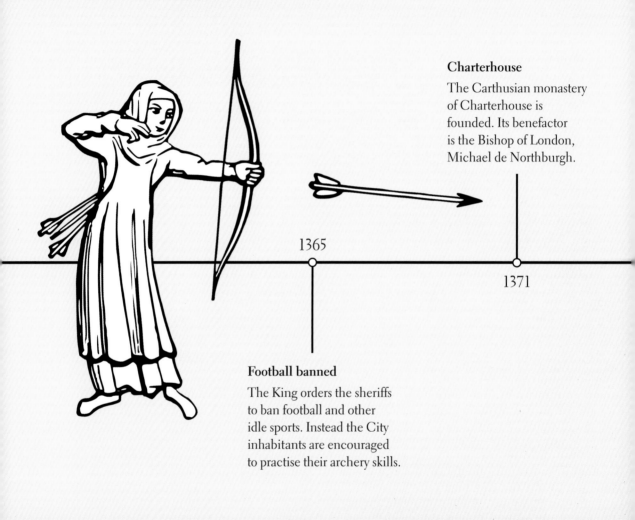

Charterhouse

The Carthusian monastery of Charterhouse is founded. Its benefactor is the Bishop of London, Michael de Northburgh.

1365

1371

Football banned

The King orders the sheriffs to ban football and other idle sports. Instead the City inhabitants are encouraged to practise their archery skills.

Chaucer's customs

Geoffrey Chaucer, later author of *The Canterbury Tales*, is appointed Comptroller of Customs for the Port of London, and moves into a dwelling over Aldgate, a City gate close to the Custom House.

1374

GEOFFREY CHAUCER
c.1340-1400
BY SIR GEORGE J. FRAMPTON, R.A.
PRESENTED BY ALDERMAN SIR REGINALD HANSON, BART. 1903

Revolting peasants

Incensed by unjust taxation, peasants from Kent and Essex march on London, ransacking buildings in the City and beheading the Archbishop of Canterbury on Tower Hill. The revolt comes to an abrupt end when one of the rebel leaders, Wat Tyler, is killed by the Lord Mayor, William Walworth, at Smithfield. Tyler's head is displayed on London Bridge.

Courting rules

The first recorded reference to what are now known as Inns of Court – associations of legal professionals to which barristers must belong before being able to practise. By common agreement, none of the four surviving inns claims to be the oldest; today, two of the remaining inns are located in the City: Middle Temple and Inner Temple.

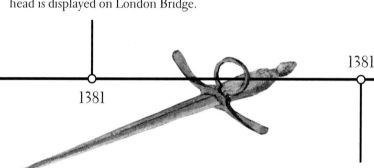

1381

1381

1388

Knollys rose

Licence is granted to Sir Robert and Constance Knollys to build a bridge over Seething Lane to connect two of their houses, situated on either side of the lane. The rent is to be one red rose rendered to the Lord Mayor at Midsummer. Although this custom continues for many years it eventually lapses, but is revived in 1924 by the Reverend 'Tubby' Clayton, of Toc H fame. In a ceremony continued by the Watermen and Lightermen's Company, a red rose is still cut each year from the public garden in Seething Lane and presented to the Lord Mayor at Mansion House.

Plagues in London

The infamous outbreaks of 1348 and 1665 are but two of almost forty to strike London in those years. A major outbreak hits roughly every 20–30 years, each killing 20 per cent of London's population. Lesser outbreaks occur in between, sometimes lasting several years.

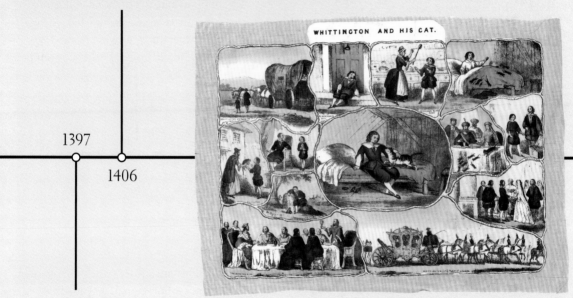

WHITTINGTON AND HIS CAT.

1397

1406

Dick Whittington

Richard Whittington, a wealthy London mercer, is appointed Mayor by the King after the previous Mayor dies in office. Whittington is elected Mayor on three further occasions. Having no heirs, his wealth is used for a number of charitable purposes, including the repair of Newgate and the foundation of a library at Guildhall. He may (or may not) have had a cat.

1411

Guildhall

Work begins to rebuild Guildhall, the centre of City government.
After twenty years the magnificent hall, 152ft long by 48ft wide,
is second only to Westminster Hall. Despite being partially
burnt in the Great Fire of 1666 and bombed in the Second
World War, much medieval fabric survives to this day.

Moorgate built
This City gate leads out to the marsh where people skate on the ice in winter.

1413

1415

1419

Cry freedom!
The daughter of Welsh freedom fighter Owain Glyndwr, Catrin and her children are captured by the English in 1409 and taken to the Tower of London. She and two of her children die in 1413 and are buried within St Swithin's Church in the City. Her burial site in St Swithin's Garden, recently remodelled and renamed Walbrook Garden, is commemorated by a memorial, unveiled in 2001, to Catrin and to all women and children who have been victims of war.

All hail to the ale!
Ale Conners inspect the quality of beer. The City has four, now largely ceremonial, who enact a legendary process: they pour the beer onto a wooden bench and, wearing leather breeches, sit in the pool. If they stick to the bench, then there's too much sugar and the beer fails. It is still conducted a few times each year, typically when a new pub or beer is introduced.

Guildhall Library

Former Mayor Richard Whittington dies in 1423 leaving a vast sum of money, part of which is used to found a library at Guildhall to serve a college of priests. Standing a few yards south-east of Guildhall, the library is a two-storey stone building, with a stone roof. The library of chained books occupies the upper floor and is staffed by at least one librarian.

1423

The Lord Mayor

In the 12th century, as part of a move towards civic independence for London, the office of Mayor was created, the first recorded incumbent being Henry Fitzailwyn in 1189. A charter of 1215 granted the citizens of London the right to 'choose to themselves every year a mayor', whom they could either remove or retain at the year's end. Today, by custom, Lord Mayors do not serve more than one term, but in the past Mayors, including Richard 'Dick' Whittington, could and did serve multiple terms in office.

The Lord Mayor is head of the Corporation of London, its chief magistrate and chairman of its two governing bodies, the Court of Aldermen and the Court of Common Council. Within the City the Mayor ranks above everyone, except the Sovereign. Other offices held in an official capacity include Admiral of the Port of London, Trustee of St Paul's Cathedral and Chancellor of City University; he also presides over Her Majesty's Commission of Lieutenancy for the City of London. During their year of office, Lord Mayors promote both the City and the UK financial services sector at home and abroad.

The election of the Mayor takes place annually on 29 September, and on the Friday preceding the second Saturday in November he is sworn into office in Guildhall in a ceremony known as the Silent Change. This symbolic transfer of the trappings of authority such as the mace, sword and purse, is carried out in total silence. The following day is Lord Mayor's Day, characterised by the Lord Mayor's Show, billed as 'the largest unrehearsed pageant in the world'. On the following Monday the Lord Mayor's Banquet is held in Guildhall, at which the Prime Minister delivers a keynote speech in front of a host of distinguished guests. During his year of office the Lord Mayor is based at Mansion House.

Colourful ex-Lord Mayors include flamboyant radical politician John Wilkes; William Beckford, a fabulously wealthy West Indian plantation owner; and Brook Watson, Mayor in 1796 who, as a 14-year-old cabin boy, lost his leg in a shark attack in Havana Harbour in 1749, as famously depicted in John Singleton Copley's painting *Watson and the Shark*. Since 1189 only two women have held the office of Mayor: Dame Mary Donaldson in 1983/84 and Dame Fiona Woolf in 2013/14.

Mercers' Maiden

The Mercers' Maiden is the symbol and coat of arms of the Mercers' Company and is first used on their seal in 1425. She adorns the exterior walls of buildings on sites belonging to the Company; one dated 1669 can still be seen in Corbet Court, off Gracechurch Street.

Vinegar beats fire

Around 2 p.m. on 1 February 1444, lightning strikes the spire of St Paul's Cathedral and it catches fire. With assistance from many citizens, the fire is quenched with vinegar.

1442

1425

1444

The Strand is paved

From the 13th century onwards, London develops into two distinct areas: Westminster, which becomes the Royal capital and centre of government; and the City of London, which becomes the centre of trade and commerce. What we now know as the Strand links the two and is the first street to be paved.

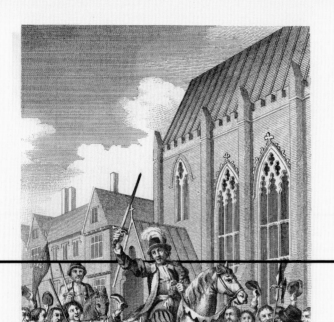

Convicting a corpse

Jack Cade leads a rebellion to protest against corruption in Henry VI's government. Londoners, initially welcoming, turn against Cade when his followers go on the rampage. They fight a pitched battle on London Bridge, and Cade flees but dies of his wounds. His corpse is returned to London, tried, convicted and ritually beheaded.

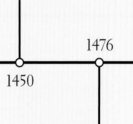

1476

1450

Caxton's printing press

Former mercer William Caxton, enthused by the new practice of printing encountered in Cologne, sets up the first printing press in England in 1476 in the precincts of Westminster Abbey.

Thomas More born in Milk Street

Thomas More becomes a lawyer, Chancellor to Henry VIII and English Catholic martyr. Following his execution in 1535, his head is displayed on London Bridge but is now interred in St Dunstan's Church, Canterbury, in the family vault of his son-in-law, William Roper.

Princes in the Tower

The 12-year-old Edward V should have been crowned King after the death of his father Edward IV. Instead he and his younger brother Richard, Duke of York, are confined to the Tower of London while their uncle takes the throne as Richard III. After this year they are never seen alive again.

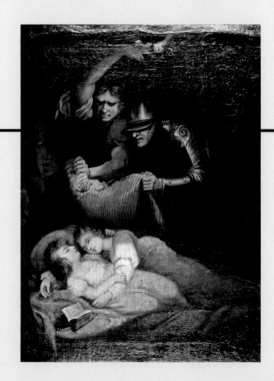

1483

1478

1483

Baynards Castle

Initially a Norman strategic fortress guarding the western City, a rebuilt Baynards Castle becomes home to the House of York in the 15th century. Here, according to Shakespeare, Richard, Duke of Gloucester, is offered and accepts the crown as Richard III in 1483. Largely destroyed during the Great Fire, parts of the building survive in Upper Thames Street until at least the 19th century.

College of Arms founded

Heraldry as the systematic use of hereditary devices on shields and seals originates early in the 12th century, and becomes a handy way of distinguishing friend from foe in battle. Heralds originally function as masters of ceremony at tournaments but are later employed as messengers of war and diplomats. Part of the royal household, the heralds are granted their first charter by Richard III in 1484 and given a house in Upper Thames Street. Heralds at the College of Arms, situated since the 17th century in Queen Victoria Street, still grant new arms and advise on the correct use of existing ones, as well as fulfilling various ceremonial functions.

1485

1484

Sweating sickness

This mysterious disease, capable of killing a healthy person within 24 hours, strikes London, felling the Lord Mayor, his successor, six aldermen and countless others within one week. Nobody knows what it was but the last cases are recorded in 1551.

TUDOR
LONDON

The Church of England

Prince Arthur, Henry VII's heir, weds Catherine of Aragon at St Paul's Cathedral, but dies five months later. In 1509 she marries his brother, Henry VIII, but bears no surviving son. Henry VIII argues for divorce, questioning whether her original marriage was consummated, but Pope Clement VII refuses. Henry VIII founds the Church of England and divorces her anyway.

1499/1500

1501

The Press comes to Fleet Street

After William Caxton's death, Wynkyn de Worde, a member of Caxton's printing team, takes over his printing business, moving it to Fleet Street in 1500. Wynkyn focuses on the mass market, producing inexpensive books with commercial appeal, and later opens a bookshop in St Paul's Churchyard.

St Paul's School

John Colet, Dean of St Paul's Cathedral, founds the Cathedral School to provide free education for 153 boys. John Milton, Samuel Pepys and Field Marshal Lord Montgomery are among the school's illustrious former pupils.

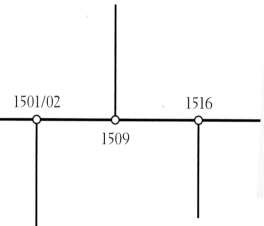

1501/02

1516

1509

Mayoral Feast

First recorded banquet at Guildhall for the Lord Mayor

At sixes and sevens

The Court of Aldermen settles long-standing disagreements between livery companies and establishes the order of precedence of the Great Twelve, the twelve richest and most prestigious guilds such as Mercers. However, the Companies of Merchant Taylors and Skinners dispute their order at six and seven. The Lord Mayor decides they should swap places each year (which continues to this day) and they became permanently 'at sixes and sevens'. Legend has it this is the source of the famous phrase.

Royal College of Physicians

Established south of St Paul's
to train and regulate doctors,
this is the oldest medical
society in the country.

Charterhouse blues

The monks of the Carthusian monastery at Charterhouse
refuse to take an oath acknowledging Henry VIII as Supreme
Head of the Church. He makes examples of several; they are
arrested, then hung, drawn and quartered at Tyburn. Among
them is the Prior of Charterhouse, John Houghton, whose
body is dismembered and displayed at various London
locations; his severed arm is placed across the gateway
into the Charterhouse as an awful warning to others.

1522

1518

1535

Moving boundaries

Thomas Cromwell, Henry VIII's chief minister,
moves from Fenchurch Street to the Austin
Friars area. In 1532 he leases two new houses
in the Friary precinct where, to maximise
his property, he relocates his neighbours'
garden fences and moves the house of
chronicler John Stow's father on rollers,
as recorded in Stow's *A Survey of London*.

King Edward's procession

A procession through the streets of the City precedes the Coronation of King Edward VI. Spectators watch from stands along Cheapside, conduits flow with wine, and a Spanish acrobat slides down a rope strung from the spire of St Paul's Cathedral to the Deanery.

1536-40

1549

1547

Dissolution of the Monasteries

In 1536, Henry VIII orders the suppression of smaller monasteries and in 1538 dissolves the larger London monasteries such as Greyfriars and Blackfriars. He confiscates their assets, turns monks and nuns out onto the streets and sells off or demolishes their buildings.

Zealots burn maypole

The vicar of St Katherine Cree preaches a sermon at Paul's Cross against heresy. Listeners become so excited they chop down and burn a maypole on Leadenhall Street. The maypole has been here so long that it has even given its name to a nearby church, St Andrew's Under the Shaft or Undershaft.

The Not-So-Beautiful Game: Football in the City

The urban City of London and large, open pitches may not seem to have much in common, and this disparity helps explain why one of the City's earliest connections with football was to ban it.

Before the rules of the game were codified in 1863, football was an unruly, violent game – very different to the slick professional operation we see today. Large throngs of people played in the streets, causing havoc and breaking windows, with limitations on the number of players and how the ball could be moved decided at a local level or between teams. This was often referred to as 'mob football'.

In 1314 Nicholas de Farndone, Mayor of London, issued a decree on behalf of Edward II:

Forasmuch as there is great noise in the city caused by hustling over large foot balls, in the fields of the public from which many evils might arise, which God forbid: we command and forbid on behalf of the king, on pain of imprisonment, such game to be used in the city in future.

Other royal bans were attempted: Edward III, Edward IV, Richard II and even Henry VIII (who ordered the first football boots on record) all tried unsuccessfully. Elizabeth I also gave it go:

No foteball player be used or suffered within the City of London and the liberties thereof upon pain of imprisonment.

Despite this, the City helped in the development of a particularly important feature of the game: legend has it that throw-ins came about because of the way players at Charterhouse School had to return the ball to the field of play through open windows in the cloister.

Beyond these City walls

Georg Hoefnagel surveys London for its earliest printed map. It shows how London has now spread well beyond the City walls.

Christ's Hospital School opens its doors

Founded by King Edward VI, Christ's Hospital School educates poor orphan children on a site next to Christchurch Greyfriars in Newgate Street. The school still exists but is now near Horsham in Sussex.

1550

1550

1552

Dutch first

Edward VI allows refugees to set up the first Dutch Protestant Church in the world, in the nave and aisles of the former monastery of Austin Friars.

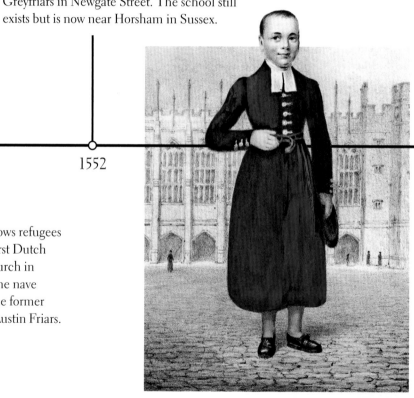

Gift of Bridewell

Built as a royal palace by Henry VIII, Bridewell is granted to the City in 1553 by Edward VI to function as a workhouse for the poor and a house of detention for 'the strumpet and idle person, for the rioter … and for the vagabond that will abide in no one place.' The name 'Bridewell' becomes an enduring byword for a prison.

1553

From Russia with love

The Company of Merchant Adventurers to New Lands
is the first institution recognisable as a modern
commercial trading venture. Tasked with finding
new trade routes with China, it runs a trading
monopoly between England and Russia, and is
renamed the Muscovy Company in 1555.

1553

Wyatt's Rebellion

Thomas Wyatt leads a protest against Queen Mary's marriage to the Spanish king, Philip II. His troops advance towards London on a wave of popular feeling, but Ludgate is locked at the last minute and Wyatt surrenders.

Old St Paul's demise

Struck by lightning or ignited from an inattentive roofer's toolkit, the spire that has towered over London for over 300 years burns down. Its demise is aided by arguments that it is God's judgment on a godless city and should be left to burn.

1553

1554

1561

Wife for sale

Thomas Sowdley, priest of St Nicholas Cole Abbey, marries during the reign of Edward VI, but Mary Tudor enforces Catholicism in 1553. To remain in post, he sells his wife to a butcher. His parishioners are unhappy.

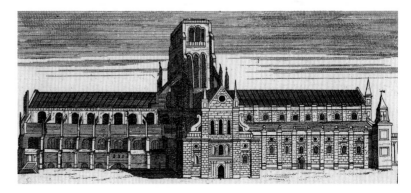

It could be you!

The first recorded lottery is drawn near the West Door of St Paul's Cathedral, with an advertised first prize of £5,000, in cash, plate and furnishings. As only one-twelfth of the hoped-for income has been obtained, the total prize money is much reduced, with the Lord Mayor and towns such as Bexley and Cambridge winning just one-third of a penny.

John Donne born in Bread Street

Poet, writer, one-time prisoner in the Fleet for marrying a minor, and later Dean of St Paul's, Donne's funerary monument in St Paul's Cathedral is the only one to survive the Great Fire of 1666 intact.

1571

1576/77

1569

1572

Royal Exchange

Wealthy merchant Thomas Gresham's Royal Exchange is officially opened by Queen Elizabeth. It is a 'place for sale of all kinde of wares, richely stored with varietie of all sorts.'

First City theatre

In 1576 Richard Farrant leases part of the old friary buildings, ostensibly as a permanent London home for the Children of the Chapel Royal, a company of child actors and singers. It becomes England's first indoor playhouse, and from 1577 the public pay to see 'rehearsals' for performances that will later be held at court. However, the crowds of playgoers offend the local residents and in 1584 the freeholder of the theatre building evicts the players and turns the theatre into tenements.

STATVA THOMAE GRESHAMI EQVITIS AVRATI
SVB PORTICV EXCAMBII REGII OCCIDENTALI POSITA

Sir Thomas Gresham dies

Gresham's death effectively leads to the foundation of Gresham College. He provides in his will that, upon the death of his widow, their house shall be used for a college in which free lectures are to be given. Gresham College still exists and still hosts free public lectures.

1579

Earthquake

In London's only recorded earthquake, masonry dislodged from the roof of Christ's Hospital kills Thomas Grey, an apprentice cobbler.

Waterworks at London Bridge

A waterwheel is installed in one of the arches of London Bridge which works a pump that can supply water to houses in many of the surrounding streets. Peter Morice, its inventor, demonstrates its efficiency by pumping water right over the steeple of St Magnus's Church.

1580

1580

1581

Captain John Smith born

A soldier and adventurer, Smith is recruited by the Virginia Company to found a settlement in America which becomes Jamestown. He is elected president, in effect Governor, of Virginia in 1608. After further American adventures he settles in London and dies in 1631. He is buried in St Sepulchre without Newgate, and a bronze statue of him stands near St Mary-le-Bow Church in Cheapside.

Lord Mayor's Show

In May 1215 King John, seeking support in the struggle with his barons, granted the City a new charter allowing annual elections on condition that the Mayor presented himself to the King or his justices at Westminster each year for approval. Gradually this annual civic riding accrued ceremonial trappings, evolving into what we know today as the Lord Mayor's Show.

Overshadowed in the early period by the pageantry associated with the Midsummer Watch shows, it was only in the late 16th century that Lord Mayor's Day came into its own. The first *printed* Lord Mayor's Show dates from 1585, and the pageants which formed so important a feature of the day and which were penned by leading playwrights like Thomas Dekker and Thomas Middleton, reached their apogee between that date and the first rumblings of the English Civil War in 1639/40. The show recommenced after the restoration of Charles II in 1660, but even then it was vulnerable to external forces; no pageants were held between 1665 and 1670 due to the Great Plague and the reconstruction of the City after the Great Fire of 1666. In 1830 riots over the Reform Bill prevented the show taking place.

As early as 1422, the Mayor and his entourage began to travel by barge to Westminster; the mayoral barge was last used in 1856. In 1752, after the reformation of the calendar and the subsequent loss of eleven days, the date of the Lord Mayor's Show, originally 29 October, was changed to 9 November. In 1959, in a bid to ease traffic congestion, it was changed by Act of Parliament to the second Saturday in November. In 1882 the procession had gone to Westminster Hall for the last time. Henceforth the Law Courts in the Strand became the scene of the mayoral presentation.

The Mansion House, home to successive Lord Mayors since 1752, and a starting point for the Lord Mayor's Show, can be visited on tours conducted by City of London guides. Many of the public rooms including the Salon and Egyptian Hall can be viewed, together with the Harold Samuel Bequest, an outstanding collection of 17th-century Dutch and Flemish paintings.

Stow's London

John Stow, a tailor living in Aldgate, publishes a history and topographical survey of London still in print today. It will become the most important history of London and an enormously valuable record of a City that will soon be almost totally destroyed in the Great Fire. Stow is buried in the Church of St Andrew Undershaft, Leadenhall Street, in 1605. The ceremony whereby the Lord Mayor places a new quill pen in the hand of John Stow's effigy takes place every year in the church on a day close to the anniversary of his death.

1598

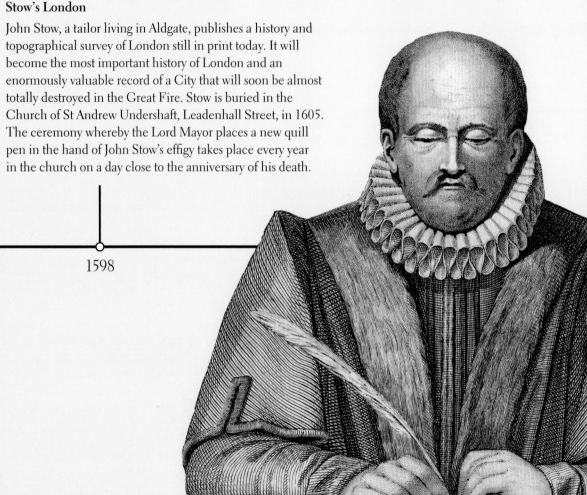

Shakespeare gets a letter

Richard Quiney writes a
letter to Shakespeare from
the Bell in Carter Lane
asking for a £30 loan. It's the
only letter to him we have.
We don't have the reply.

1599

1598

Theatre land

The first Globe
Theatre is built on
Bankside in Southwark.

Dutch spice

In 1599 the Dutch monopoly on pepper sends the price soaring from 3s to 8s a pound. London merchants form an association to develop their own trade with the East Indies. The following year the Company and Merchants of London Trading with the East Indies is granted a charter. The East India Company, as it is more commonly known, soon dominates trade with the East.

Hudson at St Ethelburga's

Henry Hudson takes communion in the tiny St Ethelburga's church before launching his ill-fated voyage to seek a Northwest Passage. Although he fails to find the Northwest Passage and indeed never returns to England, he gives his name to Hudson Bay.

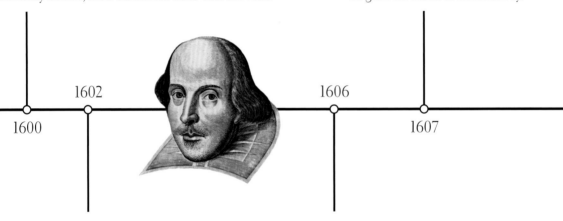

1602

1600

1606

1607

A Shakespeare premiere

The first recorded performance of *Twelfth Night* or *What You Will*, takes place in Middle Temple Hall in February.

Off to America

King James I establishes the Virginia Company by royal charter to create East Coast colonies in America. The company largely allows colonists to govern themselves, setting an important precedent concerning independence from the Crown.

The City of London Corporation –
Providing Services for the City and Beyond

Around 400,000 people come into the City to work every day and, like residents and visitors, rely on the services provided by the City of London Corporation.

The City Corporation is a uniquely diverse organisation that not only provides services you would expect from a local authority but a host of specialist ones as well. These include the City's own police force, five Thames bridges and sponsorship of several academy schools. It runs the food markets at Billingsgate, New Spitalfields and Smithfield, and is the Port Health Authority for the tidal Thames.

The City Corporation owns and manages the Barbican Centre, visitor attractions like Tower Bridge, Guildhall Art Gallery, the Roman Amphitheatre, Heritage Gallery and several public and specialist libraries across the City. Hampstead Heath and Epping Forest are the most high profile of the 11,000 acres of space under its care across London. It also works in partnership with local communities to increase skills, employment and opportunities for all Londoners.

The organisation supports and promotes London as a centre for business, especially through the work of the Lord Mayor, who heads the City Corporation and acts as an international ambassador.

STUART
LONDON

Milton born in Bread Street

John Milton, poet, statesman and writer of *Paradise Lost* is born.

Cakes and ale

On Ash Wednesday, the Stationers' Company distributes cakes and ale on the occasion of a service in the crypt of St Paul's. The custom originates under the will of Alderman John Norton who in 1612 leaves £150 for this charitable deed.

1608

1612

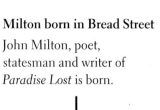

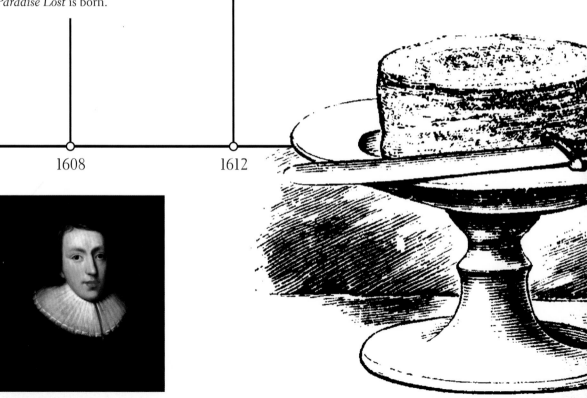

Shakespeare buys a house

On 10 March 1613 William Shakespeare purchases a property in Blackfriars for £140. The title deed, which contains one of only six 'authenticated' examples of Shakespeare's signature, is purchased for Guildhall Library in 1843 for £145 and is now regarded as one of the City's greatest treasures.

1613

1613

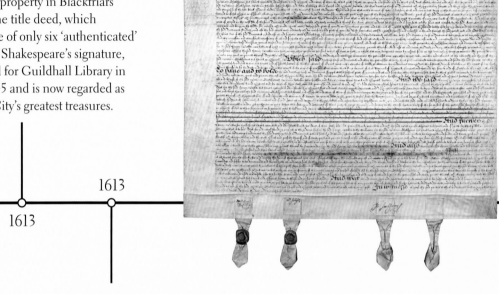

Ale to the rescue

The Globe Theatre goes up in flames during a performance of Shakespeare's *Henry VIII* when a theatrical cannon, set off during the performance, ignites the thatched roof and wooden beams. One of few surviving documents of the event lists the only casualty as a man whose burning breeches are doused with a bottle of ale.

London's oldest home

Considered the oldest lived-in house in London,
41/42 Cloth Fair was built sometime between
1597 and 1614 and remains a residence to this day.

1614

Sir Walter Raleigh

In 1592 Raleigh is briefly imprisoned in the Tower of London by Elizabeth I for marrying one of her ladies-in-waiting without her consent. In 1603 he is again imprisoned in the Tower for plotting to place Arbella Stuart on the throne, and spends the next thirteen years there during which time he writes his bestselling *The History of the World*. Released in 1616 to command an expedition to find gold in South America, he is rearrested when it fails and is beheaded in Old Palace Yard, Westminster.

1620

1618

Ollie weds Liz

Oliver Cromwell marries Elizabeth Bourchier at St Giles Cripplegate.

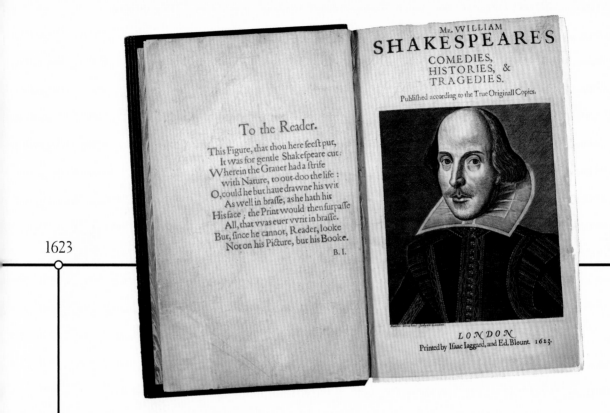

1623

The First Folio published

The First Folio is the authoritative source for
Shakespeare's plays, and is the first published
collection of his works. Guildhall Library holds
an unusually fine copy of *The First Folio*.

1623: *Shakespeare's First Folio*

The collected plays of William Shakespeare were published in 1623. Known as *The First Folio*, it has been described as the most important book in the English language. *The First Folio* contains all the traditionally accepted dramatic works of Shakespeare, except *Pericles* – the first time a book of this scale had been devoted only to dramatic works. The plays were gathered together after Shakespeare's death by his fellow players in the Company of the King's Men, John Heminges and Henry Condell. It was printed in London over a two-year period by William Jaggard and his son Isaac. It is folio in format, printed in two columns, on 908 pages. It includes a laudatory verse by Ben Jonson and the now iconic portrait of Shakespeare engraved by Martin Droeshout. Although not necessarily printed to the very highest standards of some of the great printing houses, the text is clear and legible and the paper of a medium quality. It seems likely that between 750 and 1,000 copies were printed (probably at the lower end of that scale) and some 230 survive. The Folio was issued unbound at 15s or bound in plain calf with heavy boards at £1 (the equivalent, at the time, of forty-four large loaves of bread; a single play printed in quarto cost the equivalent of one loaf). It was described by the Shakespearean scholar Sir Sidney Lee as 'the greatest contribution made in a single volume to the secular literature of any age or country'.

Because no Shakespeare play manuscripts survive and because the Folio published eighteen plays for the first time, for which it is the sole source, without it we would lack half the dramatic works – including *The Tempest*, *Macbeth*, *Julius Caesar*, *As You Like It* and *Measure for Measure*. It also offered better texts for over half the plays already published as single quartos.

Samuel Pepys

Born in Salisbury Court off
Fleet Street, Pepys works for the
navy and, over a ten-year period
from 1660-09, writes a diary which
offers a comprehensive insight
into London life and society.

1642

1632

SAMUEL PEPYS, ESQ.
Secretary of the Admiralty.
1687

MPs in hiding

Leading up to the English
Civil War, Charles I arrives at
Westminster to arrest five Members
of Parliament plotting to deny him
control of the army, but they fled to
Coleman Street, a City stronghold
of republicanism. Within eight
months, England is at war with itself.

Civil War and Cheapside Cross

Parliament orders the removal of symbols of the old faith including the demolition of several famous London crosses. Among the casualties is the Cheapside Cross, one of twelve elaborate stone monuments erected by Edward I to mark the nightly resting places of the funeral cortege of his Queen, Eleanor of Castile, on its journey from Lincoln to Westminster Abbey in 1290.

William Penn

Best known as the founder of Pennsylvania, William, son of Admiral Sir William Penn, is born near the Tower of London and baptised at All Hallows by the Tower. A convert to Quakerism, he becomes a champion of the dissenting movement and an important figure in the political and religious life of late Stuart Britain.

1643

1644

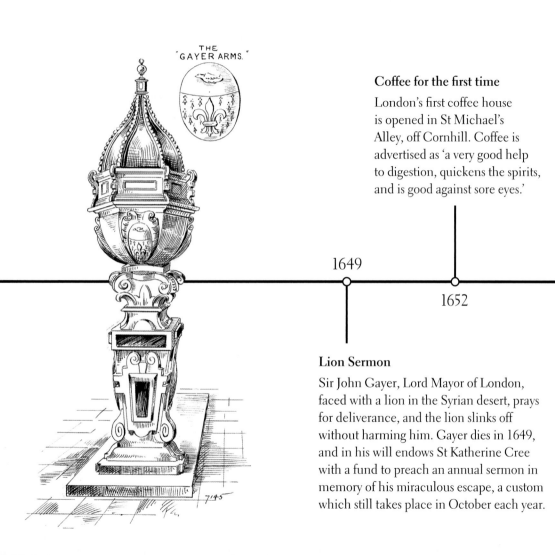

THE "GAYER ARMS."

Coffee for the first time

London's first coffee house is opened in St Michael's Alley, off Cornhill. Coffee is advertised as 'a very good help to digestion, quickens the spirits, and is good against sore eyes.'

1649

1652

Lion Sermon

Sir John Gayer, Lord Mayor of London, faced with a lion in the Syrian desert, prays for deliverance, and the lion slinks off without harming him. Gayer dies in 1649, and in his will endows St Katherine Cree with a fund to preach an annual sermon in memory of his miraculous escape, a custom which still takes place in October each year.

First cheque

Nicholas Vanacker becomes the first person to draw a cheque on a London bank for £10 on Messrs Clayton and Morris of Cornhill.

The Great Plague

Plague strikes London with full force in the summer of 1665. At its peak more than 7,000 die in a single week and by the end of the year it has claimed the lives of at least 95,000 Londoners.

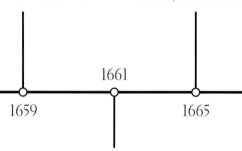

1659

1661

1665

General Letter Office

The first postmarks in the world are struck on a site now on the corner of Princes Street, birthplace of a centralised postal delivery service.

The Pestilence 1665.

1665: The Great Plague

The Great Plague of 1665 was the last major epidemic of bubonic plague to occur in England. It affected the whole country, but its impact upon the City of London, which was even then one of the greatest cities in the world, was dramatic. The cases of plague were first spotted that year in April, when a few deaths occurred in the parish of St Giles Cripplegate. By early May other cases had been discovered in nearby parishes and the authorities quickly introduced rules for quarantining infected houses. With the warmer summer weather the number of deaths began to rise to hundreds, then to thousands of deaths each week. The population was instructed to clean the streets of rubbish and edicts were issued to kill all the city's cats and dogs as they were thought to be carrying the disease. Those who could afford to leave the city did so, and the royal court moved to Oxford to avoid the contagion.

In the last week of July, the London Bill of Mortality showed 3,014 deaths, of which 2,020 had died from the plague. As the number of victims affected mounted up, burial grounds began to fill up and so pits outside the City were dug to accommodate the dead. The authorities became concerned that the number of deaths might cause public alarm and ordered that body removal and interment should take place only at night. The numbers of plague deaths peeked in September at over 7,000 a week, and then began to decline. By the end of the year the plague had virtually disappeared. Its impact has been difficult to estimate but it would seem likely that between 90,000–100,000 people died in London that year representing possibly as much as a quarter of the population.

The Great Fire of London

The fire, which broke out early in the morning of 2 September, rages for five days and is estimated to have consumed 13,200 houses, St Paul's Cathedral, 87 churches, 6 chapels, Guildhall, the Royal Exchange, the Custom House, numerous livery company halls, 3 gates, and 4 stone bridges.

1666

1672

Apothecaries Hall begins rebuilding

This is now the oldest livery hall in the City of London.

Temple Bar

Sir Christopher Wren's new western 'gate' is completed. Marking the western boundary of the City of London, it will become the ceremonial entrance to the City.

1674

1673

Traffic jam

To combat increasing congestion on London Bridge, the City introduces a rule requiring traffic to keep to the left.

The Monument

The Great Fire of 1666 is commemorated by a Doric column. Constructed of Portland stone, it is 202ft high and costs £13,450 11s 9d. Its design is a collaborative effort by Sir Christopher Wren and Robert Hooke.

1675

1677

A new St Paul's

Since 1670 Sir Christopher Wren has been working on a new design for St Paul's Cathedral. The government agrees to allow the remains of the old building to be demolished.

Fire insurance

Many householders were
ruined paying to rebuild their
homes following the Great Fire.
In response, Nicholas Barbon,
property developer and speculator,
pioneered fire insurance and
professional firefighting services.

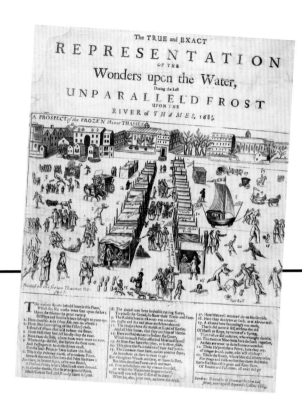

1679

1680

1684

Sweating, cupping, rubbing

London's first Turkish bath
opens in a side road off
Newgate Street, comprising
spacious rooms with tiled
walls. For 4s, a man can enjoy
sweating, cupping, shaving,
rubbing and bathing.
Women are permitted on
special days twice a week.

Frost Fair

The Thames freezes early December 1683
and lasts until February 1684. The ice is
thick enough to support the erection of
market stalls and booths, and an ox roasting.
The King, his family and members of
the court come to enjoy the festivities.

The NEW MAN after God's own heart.

And it came to pass when he came down from the Mount. Behold the skin of his face shone — Exod: 22

Alexander Pope

The poet, satirist, translator of Homer, and third most quoted writer in the *Oxford Dictionary of Quotations*, is born in Plough Court just off Lombard Street.

1688

1694

1688

Coffee house

Ship owners and maritime traders favour coffee houses rather than taverns to conduct business and Edward Lloyd's proves to be the most popular.

Hogarth

Born in Bartholomew Close, William Hogarth paints and engraves London scenes, portraits and caricatures. He also paints the murals in the entrance hall of St Bartholomew's Hospital.

BANK OF ENGLAND

Bank of England

First proposed by William Paterson in 1691, the Bank of England is now founded and granted duties on the tonnage of ships and beer, ale and liquors.

1694

18TH-
CENTURY
LONDON

Synagogue in Bevis Marks

Spanish and Portuguese Jews in London needing somewhere to worship open a new synagogue in the City of London. The architectural style reflects a Christian nonconformist chapel.

1702

1701

First daily

Elizabeth Mallet, a London printer, publishes the first daily newspaper in Britain, the *Daily Courant*, at her premises near Fleet Bridge at the end of Fleet Street. Newspapers will dominate this part of London for 300 years.

Eggs or flowers?

After writing a seditious pamphlet that parodies the government, Daniel Defoe, author of *Robinson Crusoe*, is put in the pillory on Cornhill as a punishment. Such is his popularity, the crowd throws flowers instead of rotten eggs.

1703

Carpet of flies

An August fly epidemic becomes so serious that many streets are covered deep and 'people's feet made as full an impression on them as upon thick snow.'

1710

1707

St Paul's completed

Sir Christopher Wren, aged 78, watches his son place the final stone on the summit of the cathedral. It has taken 36 years to build at a cost of £850,000, mostly raised by a tax on coal imports.

Freemasons founded

The Grand Lodge of English Freemasons first meet in a room at the Goose and Gridiron pub near St Paul's.

Bubble bursts

The first major stock market crash in Britain occurs over speculation on the price of South Sea Company stock. Thousands of investors are ruined, and new companies are barred from forming in England for decades.

1718

1717

1720

Sir John Cass

The financier endowed a school literally with his last breath; at the signing he suffered a fatal haemorrhage, staining his quill pen with blood. At Cass's annual memorial service at St Botolph Aldgate, children from the Sir John Cass Foundation School wear a red feather in remembrance.

Burglar breaks out

Jack Sheppard, aged 22, having escaped from Newgate, escapes again. Having broken through to the cell above by way of the chimney, he proceeds to break through six further doors and then lowers himself 60ft down to the ground utilising his bedclothes. He is captured and hanged.

1724

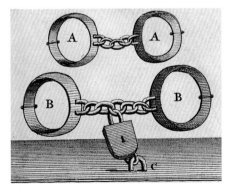

The Lower Leads

Guy's Hospital

Thomas Guy, a bookseller on Cornhill and one of few people to make a fortune from the South Sea Bubble, dies, bequeathing money to found Guy's Hospital in Southwark.

1726

1725

Molly houses

A molly house in 18th-century London is a tavern or private room where homosexual and cross-dressing men can meet and socialise. The most famous molly house in London is Mother Clap's.

The Big Picture:
The Defeat of the Floating Batteries at Gibraltar

Head to Guildhall Art Gallery and you'd be hard-pressed to miss this monster. *The Defeat of the Floating Batteries at Gibraltar* is one of the UK's largest oils at over 40 sq. m in size. It's so big, in fact, that today's Guildhall Art Gallery (opened in 1999) had to be especially designed to fit it in.

The painting is by John Singleton Copley, an American artist who was nearly driven to ruin by the enormous artwork, which was commissioned by the City of London to honour the Great Siege of Gibraltar in 1782. It took eight years to complete – six more than Copley had anticipated.

Depicting such an important victory needed careful consideration and that meant lots of important people got to view the painting and request changes: after initial consultation with military officers, for example, Copley had to re-do the entire layout. His methodical, academic style was also a cause for delay and demanded he travel across Europe to paint portraits of the featured officers before adding them to the canvas.

After it was finished, Copley erected a vast tent in Green Park and charged 1s for people to see it in an attempt to recoup costs. Among the visitors were the commissioners, who were alarmed to see a rectangular painting that wouldn't fit on the curved wall for which it had been intended. Their solution was simple: they demolished the curved wall and built a flat one.

The painting was finally hung at Guildhall in 1795, twelve years after it had been commissioned. Today, it provides a stunning backdrop to two floors in Guildhall Art Gallery, which is open daily and free to visit.

Going underground

A notorious public health hazard for centuries, the Fleet River is bricked over and Fleet Market built above.

1738

1738

1737

Down under

Born in Bread Street Ward, Arthur Philip is admiral of the first fleet of convicts which sails from Portsmouth in 1787, and thus founds Australia.

Wesley's conversion

John Wesley, the founder of Methodism, attending a prayer meeting in Aldersgate Street, feels his 'heart strangely warmed', the impetus to spend most of his life travelling and preaching.

Clock of St George the Martyr, Southwark

Made by George Clarke of Whitechapel for £90 in 1738, the clock has four dials in the steeple. Three faces are white and lit at night. The remaining black dial faces Bermondsey whose parishioners, so urban legend has it, refuse to fund the development.

1739

1738

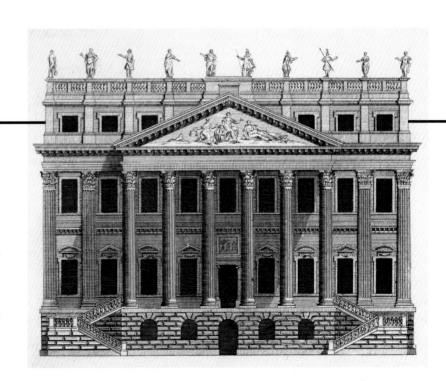

Mansion House

The Lord Mayor needs a purpose-built home to reflect the importance of the role and to entertain London merchants, many of whom, although retaining City business premises, have moved home to the suburbs.

Foundling Hospital

Philanthropist Thomas Coram founds the hospital to home, educate and care for abandoned children. Each child arrives with a memento, like a coin, thimble or other trinket, so their parents might recognise them in later years.

1741

Orange Appeal: City Bells

'Oranges and lemons…' begins the well-known English nursery rhyme. There are a few different variations (some quite gruesome, and others edited to be more suitable for children), but all start with:

'Oranges and lemons,' say the Bells of St Clement's
'You owe me five farthings,' say the Bells of St Martin's
'When will you pay me?' say the Bells of Old Bailey
'When I grow rich,' say the Bells of Shoreditch
'When will that be?' say the Bells of Stepney
'I do not know,' say the Great Bells of Bow

The bells of all six churches are suggested to be in, or close to, the City and it is thought by some that the lines of the song were originally sung to the tune of each church's bells. The churches are thought to be:

Bells of St Clement's – St Clement Eastcheap on Clement's Lane (although some believe this refers to St Clement Danes which is located in the City of Westminster, just on its border with the City of London)
Bells of St Martin's – St Martin Orgar on Martin's Lane (destroyed in the Great Fire, only the churchyard remains)

Bells of Old Bailey – St Sepulchre-without-Newgate on Holborn Viaduct and Giltspur Street
Bells of Shoreditch – St Leonard on Shoreditch High Street, just outside of the City
Bells of Stepney – St Dunstan and All Saints Stepney on Stepney High Street, east of the City
Great Bell of Bow – St Mary-le-Bow on Cheapside

The lines all correspond in some way to a feature of the relevant church – for instance, St Clement Eastcheap is near the wharf at which citrus fruits used to arrive into London, and St Martin's was in an area known in days gone by for a preponderance of money-lenders.

The Bow Bells – the last of the bells to be featured in the rhyme – are famous for many reasons: in 1392, Richard (Dick) Whittington heard them call him back to London to become Lord Mayor; to be born within the sound of them was the sign of a true Londoner or Cockney; and, during the Second World War, the BBC's World Service broadcast a recording of them as a symbol of hope to the free people of Europe.

Oranges and Lemons

Tom Thumb's Pretty Song Book is published, containing the first recorded instance of 'Oranges and Lemons', a nursery rhyme referring to City churches. There is still no agreement as to which St Clement's Church features in the rhyme.

Last execution on Tower Hill

Lord Lovat, a supporter of the Jacobite Rebellion of 1745, becomes the last person publicly beheaded in England. Shortly before his execution, a scaffold for spectators collapses, leaving twenty dead and Lovat amused.

1744

1747

Fielding's Force

John Fielding, notable English magistrate and social reformer, and his brother, novelist Henry Fielding, are instrumental in forming the Bow Street Runners, London's first professional police force.

Tragedy at the Monument

William Green, a weaver, reaches over the Monument's railings to gain a closer look at a live caged eagle suspended from the balcony. He loses his balance, falls and dies. Why an eagle is caged at the Monument is rather unclear.

1749

1750

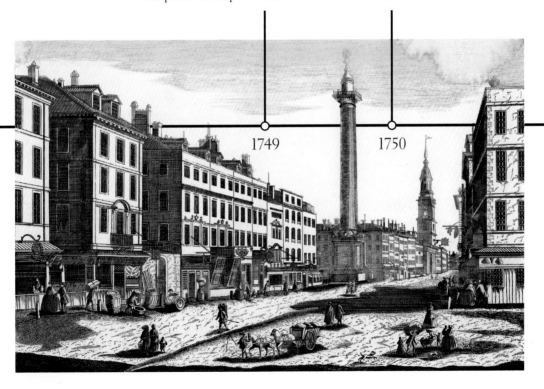

The lady vanishes

Londoner Elizabeth Canning disappears aged 19 on New Year's Day 1753, then reappears on 29 January. She claims she was kidnapped and accuses Mary Squires, who is tried and sentenced to death, but then pardoned. Subsequently, Canning is tried for perjury and transported to America. No one discovers the truth nor where Canning was those missing four weeks.

1755

1753

The standard dictionary

Dr Samuel Johnson of 17 Gough Square, off Fleet Street, publishes his *Dictionary of the English Language*. His labour of love has taken almost nine years but sets the standard by which all dictionaries are subsequently judged.

The Lord Mayor's coach

After being unsaddled by a drunken flower girl on Lord Mayor's Day in 1711, Sir Gilbert Heathcote becomes the last Lord Mayor to ride in procession on horseback. Henceforth, a coach is used. The current magnificently gilded coach is commissioned in 1757 by the incoming Lord Mayor, and made in Holborn at enormous cost.

Turtle soup

Becoming popular at City banquets, it is a feature of City celebrations for 200 years.

1757

1757

Gates razed

Aldgate, Bishopsgate, Ludgate and Cripplegate are the first City gates demolished in the City's street improvement drive.

1762

1760

No hanging signs

The proliferation of trade and shop signs hanging outside London buildings obscure each other and if not properly affixed are a health hazard. The Cities of London and Westminster now require premises to place signs flat against their walls.

Scratching Fanny of Cock Lane

A famous hoax is perpetrated in Cock Lane that fools most of London society, including Samuel Johnson. Scratching sounds of a supposedly murdered woman named Fanny terrify a household and grip Londoners' imagination, until exposed as a girl with a wooden clapper.

1762

The Cock Lane Ghost

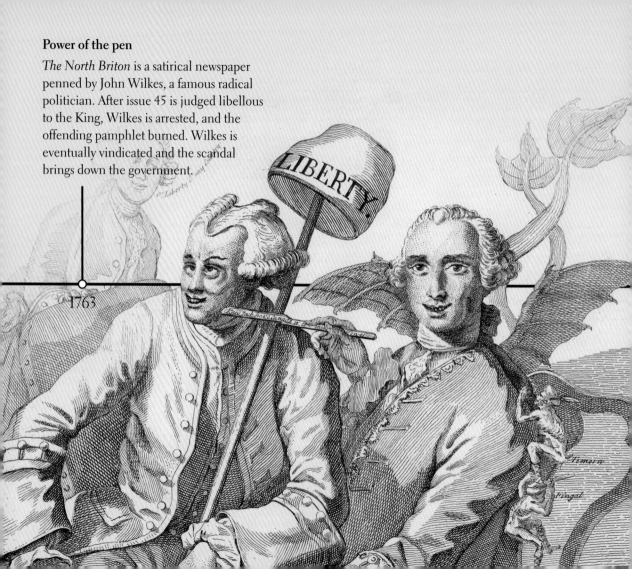

Power of the pen

The North Briton is a satirical newspaper
penned by John Wilkes, a famous radical
politician. After issue 45 is judged libellous
to the King, Wilkes is arrested, and the
offending pamphlet burned. Wilkes is
eventually vindicated and the scandal
brings down the government.

1763

Lloyd's Register of Shipping

Lloyd's Register publish their first Register of Shipping. It gives ship owners, maritime traders and insurers a factual summary of vessels they own, charter and insure.

Common Green

Robert Mylne's bridge, the first over the Thames between Blackfriars and Southwark, opens. The river's third bridge, it costs £230,000 and is painted predominantly the same green as the leather seats in the House of Commons, in contrast to Lambeth Bridge's red of the seats in the House of Lords.

1764

1769

1773

Stock Exchange

Traders in government securities and company shares or stocks take over Jonathan's Coffee House and eject the other patrons. They buy their own building in Threadneedle Street. Initially called New Jonathans, they rename it the Stock Exchange.

The City, the city or the City?

What do people mean when they say the City? The term can mean different things depending on context, and it can get confusing if a writer or speaker isn't explicit about what they're discussing. So, to be clear, the City has three popular meanings:

- It can refer to the City of London as a geographic region: the ancient City of London that is roughly one square mile in size and extends from the Thames in the south to the Barbican in the north; from the Tower in the east to the Temple in the west.

- It can refer to the City of London Corporation, the ancient government of the City of London which provides local authority services to the square mile and is the body to which aldermen, councillors, sheriffs and Lord Mayors of the City of London are elected.

- It can also be used to mean the financial services industry, thanks to the City of London's status as a popular site for headquarters of banks, law firms, auditors, insurance companies and assorted other businesses that provide financial services. When it's used in this sense, 'the City' usually includes all financial services businesses in Britain, whether they're in the geographic City of London or not.

It's also worth remembering that the city of London (without a capital 'c') is different from the City of London – it means the greater London urban area.

Confused yet? If in doubt, ask.

Gordon's Gin

Incensed by legislation granting limited new rights to Catholics, a large crowd of anti-Catholic protestors rampage through London. They burn Newgate Prison to the ground and prisoners flee. The riots climax in the destruction of Thomas Langdale's gin distillery in Holborn which explodes. The alcohol ignites and many rioters drink themselves to death.

Ode to a Nightingale

The poet John Keats is born in the Swan & Hoop Inn on Moorgate and baptised at St Botolph without Bishopsgate on 18 December 1795. A medical student at Guy's Hospital, he abandons his studies for poetry. Although dying aged 25, his reputation as one of the great Romantic poets is established.

1785

1780

1795

Daily Universal Register

Founded by coal merchant John Walter, it is retitled *The London Times* in 1788 and based in Blackfriars.

19TH-CENTURY LONDON

Nelson's burial

After a five-day state funeral procession unlike any previously bestowed upon a commoner, the body of Rear-Admiral Horatio Nelson, preserved in a barrel of brandy since his death at the Battle of Trafalgar, is laid to rest in the crypt of St Paul's Cathedral in a sarcophagus made 300 years earlier for Cardinal Wolsey.

1806

PALMAM QUI MERUIT FERAT

NILE

TRAFALGAR

City Trials and Death

In a time before the media, it was thought that dispensing justice in public was the best way to impress the populace, and as the most populous city of the realm, the City of London was very often the venue for this. Every town had stocks, a wooden bar with holes for the feet and/or hands, where miscreants would be displayed and humiliated for crimes as diverse as fraud, adultery and sedition. The City of London's once stood at Bank Junction, on the site of what is now the Mansion House, the Lord Mayor's official residence and itself home to prison cells for the detention of those who had displeased the City's authorities.

Before the construction of purpose-built courthouses, Guildhall's Great Hall was often used as a venue for high-profile trials, such as that of Lady Jane Grey in 1553, and of other players in the religious and political power struggles of the 16th and 17th centuries.

Although capital punishment is no longer allowed under British law, for many centuries it was not only practiced but was undertaken in public. The last time this occurred in the City was outside Newgate Prison (now the Central Criminal Court, known as the Old Bailey) as recently as 1868, an event to which spectators travelled using the newly built Underground! Newgate, as the chief prison of London, had been an execution site since 1768, and it's estimated over 1,000 people went to their deaths there, often in front of crowds numbering up to 100,000.

However, there were other venues where public punishment of criminals would take place. The most famous of these was Tower Hill, site of the gory and protracted executions of the great and the not-so-good which took place for over three centuries. Victims of hanging, drawing and quartering (as well as boiling, burning and just plain old beheading) included bishops, generals, noblemen, politicians, soldiers, housewives and the odd unfortunate chef.

Some executions also took place at Smithfield, most notably that of William Wallace (popularly known as Braveheart), but also those of the many victims of religious persecution, both Catholic and Protestant, whose principles were in opposition to the prevailing government of the day. It was also the scene of the murder of Wat Tyler, leader of the Peasants Revolt in 1381, by the-then Mayor of London!

There were also public trials, punishments and executions in what seem like more unlikely places, such as by St Paul's Cross next to the cathedral (some of the Gunpowder Plotters met their deaths here) and occasionally at the places that crimes themselves took place. Chaucer, for instance, when living above Aldgate, would have had to put up with a corpse hanging near his window on at least one occasion.

And there was often little peace for the corpses once life had departed them. The heads (and sometimes limbs) of executed traitors were exhibited on the top of the City's gates, most notably London Bridge, and Temple Bar when it stood in Fleet Street.

The Angel of Prisons

Elizabeth Fry visits Newgate Prison. The conditions horrify her and she introduces supervision, sewing and Bible reading. Nobility visit, prisoners engage and in 2001 she graces the £5 note.

Ice over

The Frost Fair on the frozen River Thames begins on 1 February and lasts four days. Thousands visit stalls erected on the ice and one day an elephant is led across the river below Blackfriars Bridge.

1813

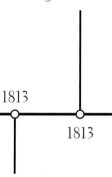

1813

1814

The great fogs

The burning of coal for domestic and industrial use contributes to a wave of terrible fogs, including one which starts on 27 December and lasts for eight days.

What the Dickens

A 10-year-old Charles Dickens arrives in London at Wood Street, near Guildhall, in a coach with passengers 'packed in like game'.

1828

1822

1829

New library

The original Guildhall Library existed between *c.* 1423 and 1549. Now a new library opens, its collections relating mainly to the City, Southwark and Middlesex. For the benefit of Members of the City Corporation and accredited students, it develops into a major reference source for London history and English local studies.

Omnibus

George Shillibeer sets up the first regular passenger bus route running from Bank to Paddington. The fare on this horse-drawn omnibus is 1*s* 6*d* for inside passengers and 1*s* for those sitting on top.

Gin palace

The City's first gin palace, Thompson & Fearon's, arrives in 1829. Their ornate decoration and counter bars influence Victorian pubs for decades. It is also notable for being on the dividing line between the City and Holborn. Legend says the line is marked by a rope across the bar, and, with different licensing laws, drinkers cross the rope at 10 p.m. to continue drinking.

1829

THESE are the *Drinks* that are sold night and day,
At the bar of the Gin-shop, so glittering and gay.

Menagerie madness

An under-keeper accidentally raises a door in the menagerie at the Tower of London allowing a lion, Bengal tiger and tigress to meet. The ensuing fight lasts half an hour; the lion succumbs to its wounds and dies a few days later.

1830

River Deep: the City's Lost Waterways

When it comes to London's rivers, few of us won't have heard of the Thames, but what of the Walbrook and the Fleet, remembered in City street names but long since covered over and forgotten?

The Walbrook was a freshwater stream running between the two hills by the Thames on which London was founded. Used to wash away animal blood from Mithraic rites at the nearby Roman temple of Mithras and to flush London's first large-scale public toilet in the 15th century, the Walbrook's past is murky. A claim supported by recent archaeological finds which include large numbers of human skulls, thought to be an offering to appease a god or victims of gladiatorial combat.

By the time of the Great Fire (1666), the Walbrook was diverted into sewers, its name living on, perhaps most aptly, in Walbrook Wharf, where the City's rubbish is taken away by barge along the Thames.

The Fleet is larger than the Walbrook and played an integral role in industrial life, turning watermills in Clerkenwell, and supplying the butchers of Smithfield and the printers of Fleet Street (to which it gives its name). Over the centuries, pollution from these industries fouled the water to such an extent that poets wrote satirical verses about its unpleasantness, and the decision was taken to cover it over, building a street on top (Farringdon Road, Farringdon Street and New Bridge Street).

Yet even when it had been buried, the steep valley proved an impediment to east–west traffic, relieved in the 1860s with the construction of the Holborn Viaduct. Standing on the viaduct, looking south towards Blackfriars Bridge, is the best place to see where the filthy Fleet once flowed, bringing 'its large tribute of dead dogs to Thames' (Alexander Pope, Dunciad).

Abridged London

King William IV and Queen Adelaide
open the new London Bridge designed by
Sir John Rennie. After a seven- year build, it is
considerably wider than its medieval predecessor.

Mrs Beeton

Isabella Mayson is born in Milk Street, off
Cheapside. She is best known for *Beeton's Book
of Household Management* which includes not
just recipes but all aspects of running a house.

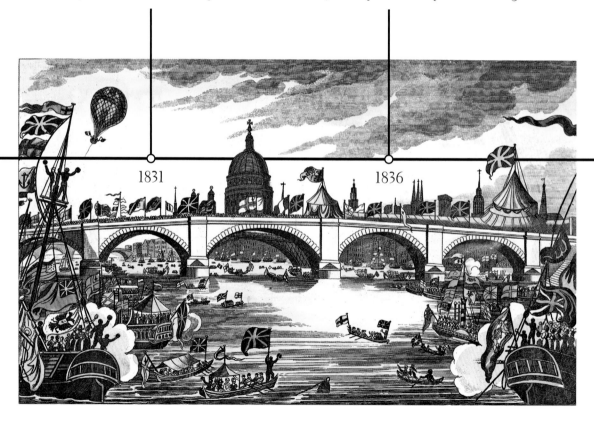

1831

1836

City station

The London & Blackwall Railway opens the first terminus in the City at Fenchurch Street. Trains are dragged from Blackwall to Minories by cable and reach Fenchurch Street under their own momentum. Gravity and helping hands from station staff ensure trains leave.

Fleet prison demolished

Fleet prisoners languish for years, unable to pay their creditors, when debt was a custodial offence. Large numbers of imprisoned priests married couples cheaply.

1844

1841

1846

YMCA

The Young Men's Christian Association is founded at a meeting held in Hitchcock & Rogers's drapery store in St Paul's Churchyard. It improves conditions of young workers living above offices of their employers.

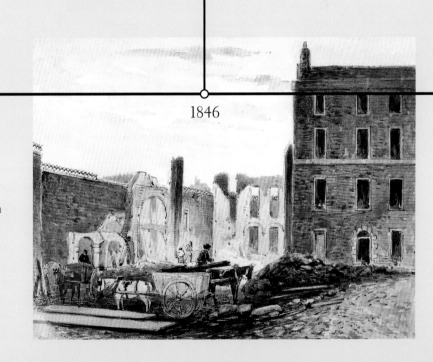

Sweeney Todd

The novel *The String of Pearls* introduces Sweeney Todd, the Demon Barber of Fleet Street, to the general public. The site of his barber's shop is still pointed out to tourists despite him being a fictional character (or is he?).

Spending a penny

The first modern public lavatory is erected at 95 Fleet Street, for men only, and discreetly called a 'public waiting room.'

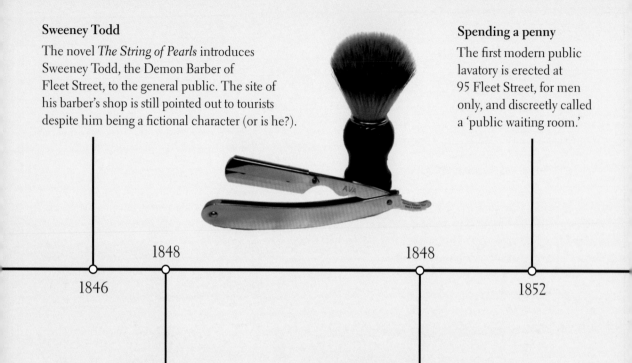

1848

1848

1846

1852

Brontë sisters

Novelists Charlotte and Anne visit their publisher George Smith in Cornhill, to disprove accusations that they are the same person.

Chopin's last performance

Frederic Chopin plays to great acclaim at Guildhall as part of the 'Grand Dress and Fancy Ball' in aid of Polish refugees. It is his last ever performance.

Fleet Street: the History of the British Press

Fleet Street was for many years the home of the British newspaper industry, and had such a strong connection that even today – a couple of decades since most of the newspapers moved out – it is still used as a collective term for the Press.

The street was an ideal location for printing. It was (and still is) the main pedestrian route between the City of London and the City of Westminster, and is next door to the legal Inns of Court and the Royal Courts of Justice: government to the west, commerce to the east, and the judiciary on the doorstep. This mix attracted plenty of passers-by and the area became a hub for conversations, discussions and gossip.

The association began when Wynkyn de Worde – an apprentice of William Caxton who brought the printing press to Britain – took over Caxton's business and set up shop in Fleet Street. The area became a literary hotspot over the centuries, attracting legendary writers like Dr Johnson (who compiled the first English dictionary, and whose house just off Fleet Street is now a museum), Charles Dickens, John Milton, William Hazlitt, Samuel Coleridge and plenty more. With its ideal location, preponderance of pubs and historic connections to printing presses and writers, Fleet Street became the natural home of the newspaper.

The *Daily Courant* was the first daily newspaper in Britain, published by the printer Elizabeth Mallet at her premises on Fleet Street. Many followed: Fleet Street and its environs were home to the *Telegraph*, the *Daily Express*, the *Daily Mail*, the *Sun*, the *News of the World*, innumerable regional papers and global news agencies like the Press Association. In its heyday, Fleet Street moved to the rhythms of the newspapers: ink-stained printers working the night shift to get the next day's news out; delivery trucks shuttling in and out of buildings carrying their papers far and wide; and journalists lunching (extensively) in the local pubs with colleagues and sources.

The legacy of the Press is still around Fleet Street: St Bride's, a Wren church whose distinctive spire is said to be the inspiration behind the tiered wedding cake, is the journalists' church, with memorials to many important figures in the Press's history and services in memory of journalists killed in the line of duty. The many pubs and wine bars around Fleet Street carry plaques to famous journalists and editors. Beautiful Art Deco buildings, out of which the great national broadsheets operated, still stand on the north of the street.

Newspapers began moving into new premises away from Fleet Street in the 1980s to save money. The last major news organisation to leave Fleet Street was Reuters, who moved out in 2005, though there are still some publishing companies with offices in the area.

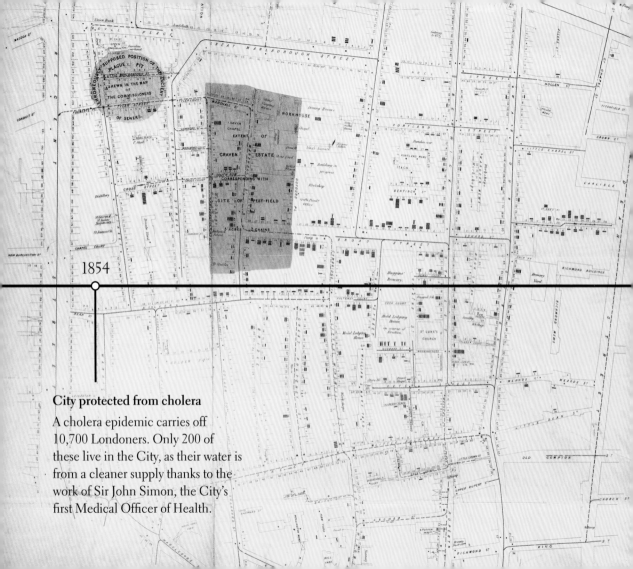

1854

City protected from cholera

A cholera epidemic carries off
10,700 Londoners. Only 200 of
these live in the City, as their water is
from a cleaner supply thanks to the
work of Sir John Simon, the City's
first Medical Officer of Health.

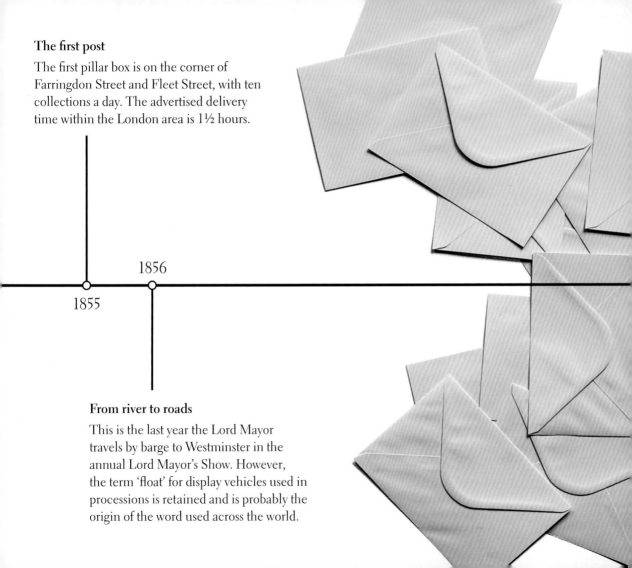

The first post

The first pillar box is on the corner of Farringdon Street and Fleet Street, with ten collections a day. The advertised delivery time within the London area is 1½ hours.

1856

1855

From river to roads

This is the last year the Lord Mayor travels by barge to Westminster in the annual Lord Mayor's Show. However, the term 'float' for display vehicles used in processions is retained and is probably the origin of the word used across the world.

City of London brings out its dead

The City's graveyards groan; overcrowded and in a state of decay, they are a risk to public health. The City of London Corporation buys land east of London in Ilford and builds the City of London Cemetery and Crematorium. The first body is interred in 1856 and the total figure approaches 1 million (among them two of Jack the Ripper's victims).

1856

First public drinking fountain

The Free Drinking Fountain Association, later the Metropolitan Drinking Fountain and Cattle Trough Association, is founded to provide clean drinking water and to further the temperance movement. It can still be seen, close to St Sepulchre's Church in Newgate Street.

1861

1859

Coal posts

These marker posts, many of which still exist, are erected following an Act of Parliament. They form a loop up to 18 miles distant from London marking points where taxes on coal are due to the City of London.

Pearly royalty

Pearly Kings and Queens are London fundraisers who decorate their 'Smother Suits' with glittering pearl buttons. The first King, and originator of the tradition, is Henry Croft who is presented with a medal by the Lord Mayor for raising significant sums for charity. Every year at Harvest Festival, Pearly Kings and Queens parade from Guildhall to St Mary-le-Bow Church.

First underground railway

The Metropolitan Railway, the world's first underground railway, opens, running between Paddington and Farringdon. In the first six months, a daily average of nearly 28,000 passengers make the 18-minute journey between Paddington and the City.

1861

1863

City Markets

From the very beginning, London's existence was dependent on commerce. The Romans built their largest forum (marketplace) north of the Alps in London.

When King Alfred reoccupied the walled city in the 9th century he laid out a classic herringbone pattern of streets leading off one wide street. That street, called Cheapside, or sometimes Westcheap from the Saxon word *cepe* for market, remains, as do many of its tributaries which over time acquired names according to what you could buy in each – Milk Street, Bread Street, Honey Lane, Poultry, Cornhill, etc. Another street further east (Eastcheap) supplied the needs of that part of the city.

There was also a livestock (and later meat) market in the Smithfield (smooth, as in flat, field) outside the City gates, a fish market at Billingsgate by London Bridge, a fruit and vegetable market in Spitalfieds (the fields outside the (ho)spital of St Mary Bethlem), and a general food market in the Leadenhall, an old lead-roofed complex sited right on top of what had once been the Roman forum. Later on, a second-hand clothes market on the eastern edge of the City became known as Petticoat Lane from the garments on offer there.

Although the Great Fire of London changed London irrevocably, and markets opened in other areas to cater for a growing city, the City's markets were still the most famous. The Billingsgate porters were famous for their foul language, Leadenhall was the adopted home of Old Tom, a goose that escaped the Christmas slaughter for thirty-seven years, and Smithfield was so busy that a new road (now Euston Road) had to be built so cattle could travel there from the west of England without trampling through the fashionable districts of the West End.

In the Victorian period, as a mark of civic pride, many of these markets had handsome covered halls designed for them, in most cases by the City Surveyor Horace Jones, also responsible for the design of Tower Bridge. And these buildings still stand, although Billingsgate has been removed to Poplar (and the building repurposed as an events venue) and the Spitalfields wholesale market is now in Vauxhall. Petticoat Lane still operates, although the Victorians changed the name of the street to Middlesex Street as they were embarrassed by the reference to ladies' undergarments.

In modern times Cheapside and Bow Lane have witnessed a resurgence in retail trade, most recently with the opening of the One New Change shopping complex behind St Paul's Cathedral.

Barnardo in Houndsditch

Thomas John Barnardo, a trainee missionary planning to go to China, is out walking one night when he finds eleven boys sleeping in the gutter in Houndsditch. Realising the extent of child homelessness and destitution in London, he begins charity work which is to become the world-famous Dr Barnardo's Homes.

1866

Abolition of public hangings at Newgate

The last person executed in public outside the gates of Newgate Prison is Michael Barrett. He is one of the men responsible for a bomb attack on the Clerkenwell House of Detention in 1867.

1868

Opening of Smithfield Market

Meat has been traded at Smithfield since the 10th century, but the present building dates back to 1868 and is designed by Sir Horace Jones, architect of Tower Bridge and Leadenhall Market.

1868

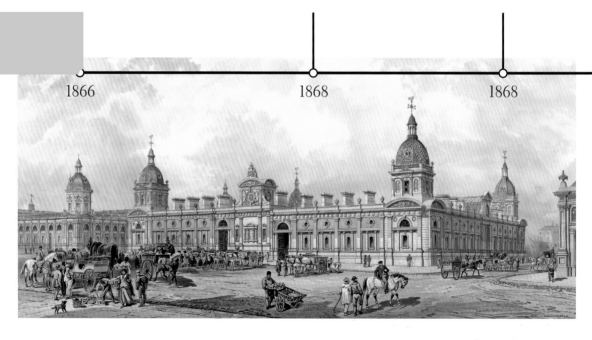

Vaults of silver below the City's streets

The Chancery Lane Safe Deposit opens and rents out strongrooms to house precious items. When silver dealers and sellers move in, it's renamed the London Silver Vaults, an impressive underground shopping arcade of precious antiques and jewellery. The thick walls and vaults have never been broken into, and even survive a direct bomb hit during the Blitz.

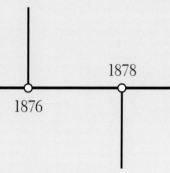

1878

1876

Forest is freed

Following years of protests the Epping Forest Act is passed, saving the remaining 6,000 acres of forest from enclosure by landowners. No longer a royal forest, it is placed in the care of the City of London Corporation stipulating that it 'shall at all times keep Epping Forest unenclosed and unbuilt on as an open space for the recreation and enjoyment of the people'.

LONDON'S TRAMWAYS

EPPING FOREST

TRAM SERVICES

FROM
BLOOMSBURY VIA ISLINGTON 81
VIA SHOREDITCH 55
LIVERPOOL ST. 57
ALDGATE 61

1880

Dragon in Fleet Street

Based on the City Arms supporters, the dragon or 'griffin' tops this memorial on Fleet Street, marking the western entrance to the City.

Leadenhall Market opens

Designed by Sir Horace Jones, the new
Leadenhall Market is a magnificent Victorian
temple to retail, with a beautifully ornate iron
roof and cobbled streets. Its striking appearance
makes it a popular film location, notably as
Diagon Alley in the Harry Potter films.

1881

Jack the Ripper

A mysterious killer, allegedly calling himself 'Jack the Ripper', murders and mutilates prostitutes in the East End during the summer and autumn of 1888. The body of one victim, Catherine Eddowes, is found in Mitre Square, just inside the eastern boundary of the City. No one is convicted of these murders and the Ripper's identity remains unknown.

1888

FINDING THE MUTILATED BODY IN MITRE SQARE .

1888: *Jack the Ripper*

Jack the Ripper was the pseudonymous murderer of at least five women, all prostitutes, in the Whitechapel area of London's East End. The case remains probably the most famous unsolved mystery in British criminal history. The five murders that are traditionally associated with the Ripper took place between August and November 1888. Mary Ann Nichols (31 August), Annie Chapman (8 September), Elizabeth Stride (30 September), Catherine Eddowes (30 September), and Mary Jane Kelly (9 November). All but one of the victims were killed whilst soliciting for customers on the street. The last victim, Mary Jane Kelly, appears to have been murdered indoors. In each instance the victim's throat was cut, and the body was usually mutilated in a manner indicating that the murderer had at least some knowledge of human anatomy.

The name 'Jack the Ripper' comes from a series of taunting notes sent to the police from a person using that name and purporting to be the murderer. Extensive newspaper coverage bestowed widespread notoriety on the Whitechapel murders and the public came increasingly to believe in a single serial killer known as 'Jack the Ripper'. The failure of the authorities to make any headway with the case led to increasing criticism of the London police. Theories and legends concerning the identity of the killer began to build up based in part on historical research but also on supposition and, on occasion, upon faked or hoaxed evidence. Barely a year goes by without a new revelation about the true identity of the Ripper which currently stands at well over 100 different individuals.

Tower Bridge

The Prince of Wales opens Tower Bridge, designed by City architect Sir Horace Jones. The Thames River remains navigable throughout the eight years of construction. The bascule bridge permits an opening of 200ft and headroom of 135ft, enough to allow access for almost all vessels to the Pool of London.

First public wireless transmission

Guglielmo Marconi convinces the General Post Office his wireless telegraphy system works by sending a message from one GPO building in St Martins le Grand to another in Carter Lane. This is seen as an effective test with St Paul's Cathedral in between and higher than both buildings.

1894

1896

1897

Diamond Jubilee

Queen Victoria arrives at the steps of St Paul's Cathedral for a service held on 22 June to commemorate her reign of sixty years. Too frail to mount the steps or even leave the carriage, the service takes place on the street.

20TH-
CENTURY
LONDON

Labour Party born

Trade unions organise the first party meeting at Congregational Memorial Hall, Farringdon Street, to fund parliamentary candidates for the working classes at a time when MPs are not paid a salary.

Bank Station brings up the bodies

Bank Underground Station is built directly below the floor of St Mary Woolnoth, a church designed by Nicholas Hawksmoor. Initially, the church is scheduled for demolition but public outcry forces a renegotiation and only the crypt is demolished. Burials at the church are removed and reinterred at the City of London Cemetery in Ilford.

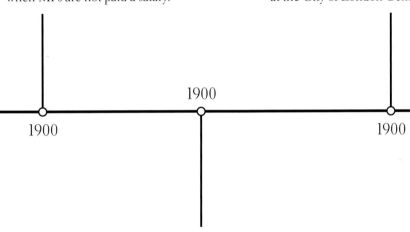

1900

1900

1900

Watts Memorial unveiled

Located in Postman's Park, George Frederick Watts' memorial to heroic self-sacrifice is a collection of simple ceramic plaques which movingly commemorate ordinary people who lost their lives saving others.

Old Bailey

The Central Criminal Court, popularly known as the Old Bailey from the street in which it is situated, opens. A 16ft figure of Justice looms 212ft above street level. Contrary to popular myth, she is not blindfolded.

A mole in the bank

Kenneth Grahame, author of *The Wind in the Willows*, works at the Bank of England during his writing career. The Bank of England Museum contains many exhibits on Grahame, and still hosts family readings of *The Wind in the Willows*.

1907

1908

Houndsditch murders

A jewellery theft and murder of three police officers by anarchists leads to a siege in Sidney Street. Ending in the death of two members of the gang, this is supposedly led by Peter Piatkow, aka 'Peter the Painter.'

1915

1910

Zeppelins over London

During the First World War, a new and terrifying threat to Londoners comes from the skies. The German airships or Zeppelins are hard to manoeuvre but still succeed in raiding London, their first bomb falling on Fenchurch Street.

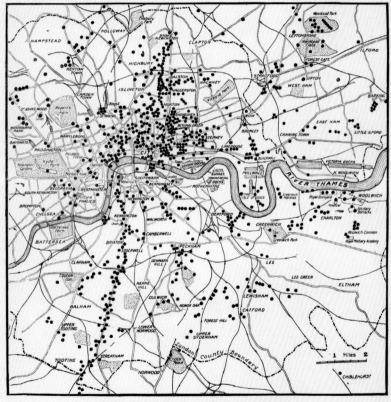

THE **Daily Mail** MAP
OF
ZEPPELIN AND AEROPLANE BOMBS ON LONDON.

Reprinted from "The Daily Mail," January 31, 1919.

Suffragette at Mansion House

In October 1920, Mansion House sees the trial and conviction of Sylvia Pankhurst for publishing what are held to be seditious articles on women's rights in *The Workers' Dreadnought*.

1927

1931

1920

Snow and a high tide

After a white Christmas deposits 2ft of snow on London, the highest tide in fifty years sweeps in, filling the Tower of London's moat.

Daily Express

The black glass and chrome exterior of the *Daily Express* building is a startling addition to Fleet Street. Its sheer modernity trumps the showy headquarters of nearby rival the *Daily Telegraph*. Hailed as the first curtain-walled building in London, its silver and gilt Art Deco lobby provides a frontage for editorial offices and a complete printing works.

1940

The Blitz

The City suffers as bombing raids begin and many historic buildings are destroyed. Despite initial resistance, London Underground agrees to seventy-nine of its stations being used as shelters during air raids. Spending the night in a tube station becomes routine for many Londoners but 40,000 civilians perish in the bombing.

Guards in the City

The 2nd Battalion Grenadier Guards return from Germany and claim their right to ancient privileges. They enter the City at Liverpool Street Station with colours flying, drums beating and bayonets fixed.

Samaritans founded

Chad Varah, rector of St Stephen Walbrook, founds the Samaritans to help those in distress with no one else to turn to.

The Queen dines in Guildhall

The Coronation Luncheon for Her Majesty Queen Elizabeth II takes place in Guildhall on 12 June 1953.

1952

1952

1953

1953

Bus jumps Tower Bridge

A watchman's mistake allows a No. 78 bus to drive onto Tower Bridge as it opens. To prevent the bus falling in the river, the driver accelerates and the bus jumps a 6ft gap between the two halves of the bridge.

Cleaner air

'Pea-souper' fog epitomises London in Hollywood movies and is a feature of London life well into the 20th century. In the Great London 'Smog' of 1952, a lethal combination of fog and smoke generated by domestic coal fires kills thousands of Londoners. The Clean Air Act of 1956 attempts to control domestic smoke pollution by introducing zones in which only smokeless fuels can be burnt.

1961

1956

Amnesty International

Barrister Peter Benenson, angered by global injustices and violations of human rights, establishes Amnesty International in his chambers at Mitre Court, Temple.

Churchill's funeral

Sir Winston Churchill dies on 24 January 1965 and is given a state funeral. His body lies in state at Westminster Hall and is then taken to St Paul's Cathedral for the funeral service.

1965

Tube disaster

Forty-three people die when a train drives at speed into the buffers at Moorgate Station. The cause is never established.

1980

1975

First skyscraper in City

The National Westminster Tower is completed. At 600ft it is the first building in the City of London taller than St Paul's Cathedral, and the tallest building in the UK for ten years. From above, the tower reflects the logo of NatWest, the bank for whom it was built.

Charles and Diana

Charles, Prince of Wales, marries Lady Diana Spencer on 29 July 1981 at St Paul's Cathedral. Widely billed as the 'wedding of the century', it is watched by an estimated global TV audience of 750 million; 2 million spectators line the route of Diana's procession into the City.

Lloyd's building

In 1979 the Richard Rogers Partnership are commissioned to design a new building for Lloyd's of London in Leadenhall Street. Although a simple rectangle in plan, it subverts convention by locating services such as lifts, toilets and fire stairs to the exterior walls, thus enhancing the drama of the twelve-storey atrium at its core.

1982

1983

1981

1986

Barbican Centre

Designed by the architects Chamberlin, Powell and Bon and officially opened by Queen Elizabeth II, this large arts complex houses a theatre, art gallery, cinemas, concert hall and library.

First female Lord Mayor

Mary Donaldson is elected Lord Mayor. After becoming a Member of the City of London Court of Common Council in 1966, she blazed a trail through the City, becoming the first female Alderman in 1975 and the first female Sheriff in 1981.

Amphitheatre

Excavations for the rebuilding of Guildhall
Art Gallery on the eastern side of Guildhall
Yard reveal an entrance and internal wall of
a Roman amphitheatre dating from AD 70,
used for military drills and gladiatorial
combat to entertain the populace.

1986

1988

1989

Big Bang deregulations

A raft of political reforms, enacted
on the same day and designed to
open financial markets as well as
remove 'old boy' networks, causes
a large and sudden increase in
financial activity in London.

The *Marchioness* disaster

A pleasure boat, the *Marchioness*,
collides with a dredger,
the *Bowbelle*, between Southwark
and Cannon Street bridges,
and fifty-one people drown.

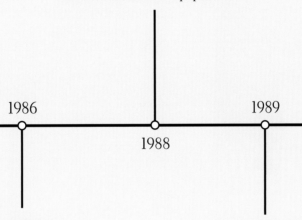

HAMPSTEAD HEATH & PARLIAMENT HILL

KEN WOOD
Showing the Art Gallery
Open Wednesdays & Fridays
1/- other days F.R.E.E.

Guildhall Art Gallery

The original Guildhall Art Gallery is established in 1885 to house and display works of art acquired by the Corporation of London since the 17th century. Burnt down during an air raid in 1941, the Gallery occupies temporary accommodation until the Corporation redevelops the site. The new Gallery, designed by Richard Gilbert Scott, is opened by Queen Elizabeth II.

1989   1992

1999

Hampstead Heath

With the demise of the Greater London Council, management of Hampstead Heath passes to the City of London Corporation. No other London borough has the expertise, experience or resources to keep the heath freely accessible. Today, the City Corporation manages around 4,500 hectares of open space around London.

Baltic Exchange

An IRA bomb destroys the Baltic Exchange's ornate headquarters. It is eventually demolished and replaced by the Swiss Re Tower, aka the Gherkin.

City Coffee Houses

'The sanctuary of health, the nursery of temperance, the delight of frugality, an academy of civility, and a free-school of ingenuity.' (Coffee-Houses Vindicated, anonymous 17th-century pamphlet)

Britain's first coffee shop opened in Oxford in 1650. Two years later, a Greek servant named Pasqua Rosee brought the new drink to the capital, opening a shop in St Michael's Alley, Cornhill. It was an overnight success and others were quick to copy. Previously, men had gathered in taverns to do business and exchange ideas. But they were often unpleasant, rowdy and – thanks to the ale – unproductive venues. Coffee, on the other hand, 'will prevent drowsiness and make one fit for business'.

Soon, intellectuals, professionals and merchants thronged to the coffee houses to debate, distribute pamphlets, do deals, smoke clay pipes and, of course, consume a drink said to resemble 'syrup of soot and essence of old shoes'. Newsletters and gazettes (the precursors of newspapers) were distributed in coffee houses and most functioned as reading rooms and notice boards announcing sales, sailings, and auctions to the businessmen who frequented them.

The best-known began to attract a distinct clientele. In 1688, Edward Lloyd's coffee house on Tower Street earned a reputation as the place to go for marine insurance. It later evolved into world-famous insurance market, Lloyd's of London. In 1698, the owner of Jonathan's coffee house in Exchange Alley began to issue a list of stock and commodity prices called 'The Course of the Exchange and other things', so starting the London Stock Exchange. Auction houses Sotherby's and Christie's have their origins in coffee houses.

Lloyd's Coffee House was opened by Edward Lloyd (c. 1648–15 February 1713), originally on Tower Street in around 1688. The establishment was a popular place for sailors, merchants and shipowners, and Lloyd catered to them with reliable shipping news. The shipping industry community frequented the place to discuss insurance deals among themselves. The dealing that took place led to the establishment of the insurance market Lloyd's of London, Lloyd's Register and several related shipping and insurance businesses.

Just after Christmas 1691, the coffee shop relocated to Lombard Street. Merchants continued to discuss insurance matters here until 1774, long after Lloyd's death in 1713, when the participating members of the insurance arrangement formed a committee and moved to the Royal Exchange on Cornhill as the Society of Lloyd's.

The 17th-century original shop frontage of Lloyd's Coffee House is owned by Lloyd's of London and has been re-erected on display at the National Maritime Museum. A blue plaque in Lombard Street commemorates the coffee house's second location (now occupied at ground level by Sainsbury's supermarket).

21ST-
CENTURY
LONDON

Wobbly Bridge

The Millennium Bridge is part of the nationwide celebrations for the year 2000. In its first two days, unexpected swaying leads to it being nicknamed 'the wobbly bridge'. It is closed for engineering and testing, and reopens without a wobble.

2002

2000

Golden Jubilee

Queen Elizabeth II's Golden Jubilee, marking fifty years on the throne, sees her attend a service in St Paul's Cathedral on 4 June, followed by lunch and a speech at Guildhall.

Temple Bar returns to the City

After languishing at Theobalds Park for many years, Temple Bar, a former gateway to the City, is re-erected in its new home at Paternoster Square.

Gherkin adds spice

Designed by Norman Foster, the Swiss Re Tower, fondly nicknamed the Gherkin, is one of the most iconic buildings in London. Its official name is '30 St Mary Axe', named after the street in which it stands.

2007

2004

2004

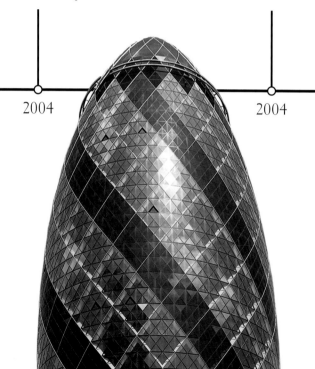

City of London Information Centre

This innovative building is designed by Make Architects, replacing its predecessor that has given fifty years' unbroken visitor service to the City of London.

Protestors occupy St Paul's

In the wake of financial crises and an era of economic austerity, protests on inequality and banking practices spring up across the world. In London, protestors attempt to gather in Paternoster Square, home of the London Stock Exchange, but are refused entry to privately owned land. Instead, they camp outside St Paul's Cathedral to protest, issue think-pieces and establish a community for over four months.

Long Live The Queen

The national service of thanksgiving is held at St Paul's Cathedral on 10 June 2016, to mark Her Majesty The Queen's 90th birthday and is followed by a reception at Guildhall.

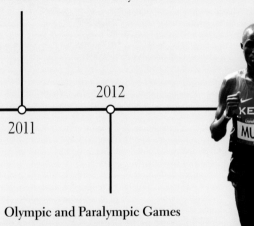

2012

2011

2016

Olympic and Paralympic Games

The Games return to London for the first time since 1948, and the City is an official 'host authority', with the marathon runners passing directly in front of Guildhall.

Also from The History Press

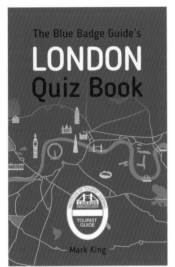